Peacemaking
for Families

FOCUS ON THE FAMILY®

Peacemaking for Families

A Biblical Guide to Managing Conflict in Your Home

Ken Sande
with Tom Raabe

TYNDALE

Tyndale House Publishers, Inc.
Wheaton, Illinois

Peacemaking for Families
Copyright © 2002 by Peacemaker Ministries
All rights reserved. International copyright secured.

ISBN: 1-58997-006-3

A Focus on the Family book published by
Tyndale House Publishers, Wheaton, Illinois 60189

Focus on the Family books are available at special quantity discounts when purchased in bulk by corporations, organizations, churches, or groups. Special
imprints, messages, and excerpts can be produced to meet your needs. For more
information, contact: Resource Sales Group, Focus on the Family, P.O. Box
15379, Colorado Springs, CO 80935; or phone (800) 932-9123.

Editor: Kathy Davis
Cover Design: Lovgren Marketing Group
Cover Photo: Chartier Studio

Library of Congress Cataloging-in-Publication Data

Sande, Ken.
  Peacemaking for families : a biblical guide to managing conflict in your home /
Ken Sande with Tom Raabe.
     p. cm.
Includes bibliographical references (p.   ).
  ISBN 1-58997-006-3
1. Family—Religious life. 2. Conflict management—Religious aspects—
Christianity. I. Raabe, Tom II. Title.
  BV4526.2 .S25 2002
  248.4—dc21
                                                    2002006714
Printed in the United States of America
2 3 4 5 6 7 8 9 / 08 07 06 05 04 03 02

To Corlette, Megan, and Jeff,
who have modeled peacemaking to me in daily life
and blessed me countless times with the gift of forgiveness

∎ ∎ ∎

TABLE OF CONTENTS

PREFACE

My family has proven to be the perfect place to learn peacemaking. Although we love each other dearly, our daily contact with one another sets the stage for disappointment and irritation, which often results in conflict. In fact, just before I finished this book, my eight-year-old son lovingly confronted me about how I was handling a conflict with my wife!

Like most other people, my family has found that there are three ways we can handle the conflicts of normal family life. We can be *peace-fakers,* denying that we have problems, always giving in, or becoming distant from family members. We can be *peace-breakers,* relying on manipulation, a sharp tongue, or overt anger to compel others to give in to our wishes. Both of these approaches can wreak havoc on families, reducing them to superficial coexistence or burned-out battlegrounds.

Our third option is to use the conflicts of family life to become *peacemakers,* drawing on God's grace and practicing the powerful peacemaking principles He has given to us in His Word. This approach may require a lot of work and change, but it is the surest way to preserve your marriage and see your family mature in love, in character, and in its witness for Christ.

This book is designed to encourage and equip you to be a peacemaker in your family. As the president of Peacemaker® Ministries since 1982, I have tested these principles in hundreds of conflicts, ranging from troubled families to bitter divorces and multi-million dollar lawsuits. More importantly, I have had to practice these principles over and over again in my own family, which struggles with sin and conflict like everyone else's family and is grateful every day for the reconciling power of Jesus Christ.

I previously described these principles in my book, *The Peacemaker: A Biblical Guide to Resolving Personal Conflicts* (Baker Books, 2nd Ed. 1997). That book provides a comprehensive and detailed discussion of how to resolve a wide range of conflicts, whether in the family, workplace, church, or courtroom. It still serves as the primary conflict resolution textbook for our ministry, which is now training peacemakers, reconcilers, and Certified Christian Conciliators™ around the world (see Appendices C-E).

In this book, I will focus exclusively and in more detail on the family. We will consider how to bring God's peacemaking promises and commands to bear on the conflicts that arise between husbands and wives, parents and children, and extended families.

In chapters 1-7, we will look at ways to resolve marital strife by identifying the root causes of our conflicts and laying them to rest through sincere confession, loving confrontation, and genuine forgiveness. In chapters 8-9 we will dive into the marvelous world of conflict with children. We will learn creative methods to resolve tensions with and between our children, and also explore ways to use the conflicts of daily life as opportunities to equip our children to succeed in their friendships, marriages, and careers by being effective peacemakers.

In chapter 10, we expand our focus and consider the challenges and opportunities of resolving conflict with parents or adult siblings. We look at ways to get help for a troubled marriage in chapter 11. Finally, in the last chapter we identify ways that you can build safeguards into your marriage in order to improve your ability to prevent or resolve future conflicts that can destroy the most precious relationships in your life.

As you will see, these principles are remarkably simple and easy to understand. Applying them is another thing! It can take quite a bit of work to put off our old habits of resolving conflict and put on God's peacemaking ways. But it is worth the effort. As you learn to be a peacemaker, you can guard your family from destructive conflict, deepen your love and intimacy with your spouse, and provide your children with a solid foundation for life. Most importantly, you can provide the world with a compelling witness to the reconciling power of Jesus Christ.

For his glory and the good of those you love, Tom and I hope and pray that this book will inspire and equip you to be a peacemaker in your family.

Ken Sande

Part 1

FAMILIES
THAT FIGHT

∎ ∎ ∎

1

Marriage Means Conflict

It was 7:30 P.M. when Steve cautiously turned the knob on his front door and slipped into the house. He paused in the entryway to look for signs of life—for his wife, Julie, sitting in the front room reading or watching TV, for his children, Josh and Tori, hunched over their homework at the dining room table. Seeing no one, he headed quickly for the hallway, which led to the refuge of the master bedroom. But before he could complete his escape, Julie emerged from the kitchen, hands on hips, to block his path.

"Finally, he's home!" she said.

Steve grunted, veering to slip past his wife.

"You said six." Julie moved over a step to cut him off.

"I got tied up."

"Third time this week you've gotten 'tied up.'" She delivered the last two words with air quotes and a sneer.

"The Hellman people called at 5:30. They're our best clients. You expect me to walk away from *them*?"

Julie snorted. "You'll have to get your own dinner."

"I picked up something on the way home," Steve said. He dropped his shoulder and sidled past her and headed for the bedroom, loosening his tie as he walked and hoping he was not being followed. If everything went his way—that is, if Julie did not insist on putting him through a blow-by-blow replay of her and the kids' day—he would quickly change clothes and sneak into the den to do more paperwork. Or he'd flee to the garage, where if he didn't have anything to do he'd find something. He'd rearranged the tool pegboard six times in the past month alone.

When he emerged from the walk-in closet, he was tucking one of his casual shirts into his jeans. Julie was sitting at her vanity facing him.

"Guess what your son did today?" she said.

He looked at her arms, crossed like a barricade on her chest, and shook his head.

"He brought home a B minus on yesterday's big math test."

Steve's eyebrows shot up. "Josh had a big math test yesterday?"

"Some dad you are! It's all he's been talking about for the past three days."

"I guess it didn't register," Steve said. He zipped and buttoned his jeans and sat on the edge of the bed, a position that indicated interest but also afforded him a perch from which to flee the scene the moment the conversation lagged. "Where's he now?"

"In his room. And he'd better be studying his math!"

"He didn't try to do well on the test?"

"He couldn't have. Our son is *not* a B-minus student."

"Maybe he didn't understand the material."

"Impossible. He and I reviewed it for two hours the night before last."

"Well, maybe he had a bad day. Kids have bad days too, you know. You can't punish the boy for that."

Julie snorted. "Why do you always manage to take the kids' side in these matters, Steve? How can you, who didn't even *know* he had a test, immediately side with Josh?"

In the interest of family peace, Steve left Julie's question unanswered. "And Tori," he said, "is she in her room too?"

"Thursday night is gymnastics night," Julie said curtly. "You know that."

"Oh, right. Thursday night is gymnastics. I get confused sometimes."

"She was in a foul mood this morning when I took her to school. She was still in a funk after school when I picked her up for swim training. She and Josh got into it at supper. And she didn't even say goodbye to me when Mrs. Browning picked her up for gymnastics."

Steve gave her his what-can-you-do shrug.

"I'm worried about her," Julie said. "She's been so *sullen* lately."

"Well, she's probably overtired. You've got her in a lot of stuff."

Julie's eyes flashed angrily. "Oh, great! And now that's my fault too? I'm only trying to allow her to develop her God-given abilities in as many activities as possible. I always thought that was a *good* thing."

"All I'm saying is she's got something every night, it seems."

Julie stood. "And all I'm saying is, it would really help me out if I could count on your support with the children. Or, at a minimum, if you were around once in a while so we could discuss the children's lives and how best to bring them up."

"You know I'm very busy at work these days, Julie."

"I can't remember you not being busy."

"It's been absolutely crazy down there."

"Tell me one thing, Steve. Please tell me when it will *not* be crazy down there? Next week? The week after that? When?"

Steve had no answer to that.

"It's *always* crazy down there, Steve. So crazy you don't have any time for your family. You come home at 7:30—if we're lucky. And when you are home, it's like you might as well not be. If your mind isn't off on a work project somewhere, you run off to the den to do more work the minute you get home or you trot out to the garage to do who-knows-what. I have to corral you in the bedroom just to talk to you."

Steve paused to rally his forces. When she attacked his work, she attacked him. He would not let that slide—peace or no peace. "I work hard, Julie," he said, his voice rising, "because that's what God calls me to do. You make it out to be a crime that I'm committed to my job. We should both be thankful that the Lord has led me to a vocation I'm good at and that I enjoy."

"No, what's a crime is the way you ignore your wife and kids. God is not commanding you to be so wrapped up in your work that you pay hardly any attention to us. That's the crime, Steve."

Steve jumped to his feet and jabbed a finger at his wife. "Well, I didn't hear you complaining when I bought you the new minivan. And the new living room set—where do you think the four thousand dollars for that came from?"

"All we want is a *little* of your precious time, Steve. Just a teeny tiny bit of your attention."

"And the tuition for the kids' school. And the fees for all this *stuff*"—Steve practically spat out the word—"you've got them in. And clothes! And spending money!"

"And who do *you* think is raising these kids? Carting them to their activities? Being *interested* in their—"

"That's the point, Julie!" Steve was shouting now. "You wouldn't be doing any of that without my paycheck."

"Well, maybe we ought to start ignoring you, too. Just like you ignore us," Julie shouted back.

"I'd sure be a lot happier if *you* did anyhow."

"What does *that* mean?"

"You are on my back constantly! It never stops. You nag and you nag and you nag!"

"Well, you are a poor excuse for a Christian father, that's all I can say."

Steve started for the bedroom door. "In fact, I'm going to let you start ignoring me right now." He bolted down the hallway.

Julie followed. "Where are you going?"

"Out."

"Where?"

Steve was at the front door. "Somewhere where you aren't!"

■ ■ ■

Conflict like this was not what Steve and Julie had in mind when they tied the knot a dozen years earlier. Both were Christians, both saw married life as God's blessing on His human creation, and both harbored visions of domestic tranquility. Steve had dreamed of being a dependable breadwinner and a loving husband, an integral part of a closely knit family unit who was *there* for his wife and kids. Julie saw herself as a supportive and loving wife, buttressing her husband in his vocation and becoming intimately—and meaningfully—involved in her children's daily lives.

They were like millions of Christian couples embarking upon a lifelong commitment to each other. But, like so many other couples, at some point in their married life conflict arose to cloud their sunny prospects.

Initially their conflicts were fairly minor, and they were able to forgive each other by drawing on the reservoir of good will that God gives most newlyweds. But when that reservoir dried up, their conflicts became more intense and the damage harder to repair. Sometimes they ended up in shouting matches, saying things they never dreamed would pass their lips and leaving wounds that never seemed to fully heal. At other times they would exchange barbs in a more restrained way, avoid each other for the rest of the day, and retreat in cold silence to their respective sides of the bed at night.

In either case, when they awoke the next morning, the preceding evening's conflict was still in the air. To avoid its toxic vapors, they were cool toward each other, talking about safe and superficial topics and pretending nothing had happened the night before. As time passed, Julie increasingly stuffed her fears and frustrations deep inside her heart and Steve seldom shared his dreams with his wife. They both knew the intimacy that had blessed their marriage in the beginning had evaporated.

Their marriage was becoming a living hell. Sometimes it was intense and angry; at other times it was relatively polite, even strangely comfortable (there's some comfort in routine and knowing what to expect, even if it's destructive). But it was a hell nonetheless, and with each passing day, it grew less and less like the marriage of their dreams. Neither of them knew how to break free from the downward spiral.

THE SLIPPERY SLOPE OF CONFLICT

Sadly, Steve and Julie's responses to conflict are all too common among married couples, even Christian couples. In spite of their faith, they had developed the habit of reacting to conflict in unbiblical and destructive ways.

There are three basic ways that people respond to conflict. These responses may be arranged on a curve or "slippery slope" that resembles an icy hill with two rapidly declining sides. On the left side of the hill are escape responses, on the right side are attack responses, and holding the high ground are peacemaking responses.[1]

Escape Responses

Escape and attack responses are almost always destructive to relationships. The escape responses to conflict are favored by those who are more interested in avoiding a conflict than in resolving it. Escape responses are generally directed inward; they are usually all about "me." Escapers are looking for what is easy, convenient, or nonthreatening for themselves. They often dread confrontation. They are usually more concerned about appearances than reality, and may be thought of as "peacefakers."

Escape responses are of three increasingly serious types. Many people live in *denial*. They simply pretend that the problem doesn't exist, or they refuse to engage and properly resolve it. The relief denial brings is almost always temporary. When problems are not properly addressed, they usually get worse in the long run.

When denial doesn't work, people often resort to *flight*. They turn on their heels and run from the conflict, escaping to the garage, ending a friendship, quitting a job, transferring out of a church, or in a family setting, filing for divorce. Flight is legitimate in extreme situations when there is danger of serious harm, such as physical or sexual abuse, and a constructive resolution of a problem is not possible at the moment. In most cases, however, flight only postpones a proper solution to a problem.

Tragically, some people lose all hope of resolving a conflict and seek the ultimate escape—*suicide*. It goes without saying that this method of handling conflict is never the right way.

Attack Responses

On the other side of the slippery slope, we find the attack responses to conflict. These responses are employed by those more interested in winning a fight than preserving a relationship. Conflict for these folks is an opportunity to assert their rights, to control others, or to take advantage of their situation. Interestingly, not only the strong and confident among us opt for this mode of conflict "resolution," but the weak, insecure, and vulnerable do as well. Attackers are not focused on "me" as escapers are, but on "you"—they blame their spouse and expect him or her to solve the problem. Attackers are often "peacebreakers," willing to sacrifice relationships and domestic harmony to get what they want.

Attack responses also come in three sorts. *Assault*, the first attack response, usually involves verbal attacks: harsh criticism, nagging, slander, angry words, or threats. Tragically, it sometimes expands to include physical hostility as well. Whether verbal or physical, attack responses invariably worsen the conflict.

Litigation—taking the matter to court—is another attack response that Christians often use, even though the Bible forbids us to sue each other (1 Corinthians 6:1-8). Litigation can involve a battle over a parent's estate, a divorce action, or an ongoing legal struggle for visitation or custody of a child. The legal system can wreak havoc on personal relationships, and children are often the ones who suffer the most.

Murder is the most extreme attack response. Although most Christians would not murder someone physically, many of them commit another kind of murder on a regular basis. In Matthew 5:21-22, Jesus teaches that if we harbor anger or hatred in our hearts toward someone else, we are guilty of murder in God's eyes. By this definition, many of the conflicts that go on in Christian homes result in repeated murder. Without repentance, these serial "murders" often kill a marriage.

In prolonged conflicts, many people vacillate back and forth between the attack and escape responses. They may seek to escape at first, but when they are cornered or attacked, they turn the tables and move into the attack zone themselves. Others may initially assume the attack mode, but when they are rebuffed or counterattacked, they throw up their hands and retreat. Sadly, it is not unusual to see a married couple alternate back and forth repeatedly between these responses, attacking and retreating in an agonizing dance of destructive conflict.

In the illustration above, Steve may vaguely realize that he and Julie have problems, but for him they are remote. Out of sight is out of mind for Steve. When he's at the office, the problem is miles away, both physically and mentally. Returning home from work means he has to think about it again. And when his wife thrusts it in his face, he tries to make it go away. Only when his job is impugned does he take a stand.

Julie, on the other hand, easily goes into attack mode because she is living with the conflict on a daily basis. Her world is her kids, whom she's around constantly, and when they misbehave or otherwise displease her, she feels it acutely and immediately. And so she takes an aggressive stance with her husband. She *wants* the conflict to be solved in her favor, or at least to get relief from her daily turmoil. Only when she sees the discussion bearing no fruit, indeed, assuming a familiar pattern—Steve not only refuses to relent, he fights back—does she flee.

Couples trapped in the cycle of attack and escape pay a heavy price. They spend considerable time and effort fighting their battles, and are drained by these fights emotionally and physically. They fail to find lasting solutions to their difficulties. There is usually severe "collateral" damage— their children, close friends, and relatives often suffer as well. And the end result, when it comes, is almost invariably negative. At least one of the partners, and oftentimes both, will find the resolution unsatisfactory. In short, couples who respond to conflict with escape and attack can usually expect to lose intimacy and grow further and further apart.

Peacemaking Responses

The good news is there's a third way to handle conflict, a better way. This way is not about "me," as escaping is, nor about "you," as attacking is, but about "us." Rather than giving in to "peacefaking" or "peacebreaking," this way is all about "peacemaking." And its result is not the end of a relationship but the *healing and strengthening* of that relationship. We will briefly introduce these responses now, then discuss them in more detail in the following chapters.

Returning to our illustration of the slippery slope, we see that moving from left to right over the crown of the hill are the three personal peacemaking responses. In most situations, couples may carry out these responses personally and privately, with no intervention from others.

First, one may resolve a conflict by simply, and consciously, *overlooking* the offense and offering immediate forgiveness. Many disputes are so insignificant that they should be resolved in this way, a way the Bible commends (see Proverbs 12:16; 17:14; 19:11).

Some conflicts are too significant to overlook, however. When important personal or relational issues are at stake, we should resolve them through *discussion*, that is, confession or loving confrontation. This, in turn, opens the door to forgiveness and reconciliation. Jesus repeatedly affirms this method for resolving interpersonal troubles (see Matthew 5:23-24; 7:3-5; 18:15).

When a dispute involves substantive issues—matters relating to money, property, or other rights—then we should engage in *negotiation*. This involves discussing each side's concerns and interests and working together to find a mutually satisfactory solution (see Philippians 2:4).

Unfortunately, not all disputes can be resolved privately; some, after repeated unsuccessful private efforts, require the involvement of other people from your church or community. There are three ways to get help in resolving a dispute.

First, you may seek *individual counseling* from a spiritually mature adviser who may be able to help you see ways that you can communicate more effectively with your spouse and still resolve your differences in private (Proverbs 13:10). Second, you and your spouse may seek *joint counseling* or *mediation*, which involves meeting together with one or more counselors who assist you in communicating and finding meaningful solutions to your differences (Matthew 18:16). Third, if your spouse won't respond to counseling and persists in sinful behavior that threatens your marriage, you may appeal to your church to exercise redemptive *church discipline* to promote repentance and restore your relationship (Matthew 18:17).

■ ■ ■

As the Scripture citations given above indicate, God commands us not to resolve our conflicts through escaping or attacking, which almost always result in bruised or broken relationships. Instead, He graciously teaches us powerful peacemaking responses that we can use to resolve the day-to-day conflicts that arise in our families.

But God does more than just lay out a process for resolving conflict. He delights to work in us and through us as we rely on His promises and obey His commands for peacemaking. At the same time, He is deeply committed to helping us understand the root causes of our conflicts and changing the attitudes and habits that threaten our relationships. In short, God is eager to display the wonders of the gospel in the midst of our marital and family conflicts so that He can reveal the life-changing power of His Son, Jesus Christ.

In the following chapters we will explore ways that we can draw on this power as we apply God's peacemaking principles to preserve the precious relationships in our families and bring glory and honor to our Lord.

AS YOU GROW

If you want to grow as a peacemaker, you need to take an honest look at how you naturally respond to conflict. You can begin by reflecting on the following questions. If you want to gain an even better appraisal of yourself, share your answers with your spouse and ask for his or her candid feedback. This may stir up some uncomfortable revelations, but it can also show you where you need to grow. If you respond to your spouse's insights and suggestions with humility, he or she may be inspired to go through a similar process of self-examination.

1. When you were a child, how did your parents typically respond to conflict? (Refer specifically to one or more of the responses on the slippery slope.) How have your parents' responses to conflict carried over into your life?

2. If someone were to ask your spouse which of the slippery slope responses to conflict you typically use, what would he or she say? What would your children say?

3. Think of a recent conflict with your spouse or children that you did not handle as well as you wish you had. Describe the progression of the conflict, referring to specific conflict responses on the slippery slope. How do you think your spouse or children felt as a result of your various responses? How did they react to your responses?

4. When you are in a conflict with people outside your family, do you respond differently than you do with your family? If so, why? If your family notices a difference, how do you think that makes them feel?

5. As your children watch your example, are they learning to respond to conflict as peacemakers, or are they learning to be peacefakers or peacebreakers? What do you want to do in the days ahead, with God's help, to be a better example to them?

2

Getting to the Heart of Conflict

Steve and Julie have been in a downward spiral for months. Whenever Steve manages to pull himself away from the office, he tries to be sympathetic to his wife when she complains about her life or their kids' lives. But he usually ends up making excuses for the kids or complaining about how Julie is handling them. This provokes Julie to become defensive and angry. How could he be so understanding of the children and so critical of her? Sometimes she flees in tears, but usually she stays and fights, laying out Steve's shortcomings as a husband and father.

The first step in breaking out of this downward spiral is for them to acknowledge they are handling conflict in a destructive way. Steve needs to recognize that he has an aversion to confrontation, so he usually tries to avoid conflict through denial. Julie has to face the fact that although she is more willing to put problems on the table, her sharp tongue often precipitates a tense if not angry conversation. And both need to see that once they have vented their anger toward each other, they often give up on a solution and escape from each other through denial or flight.

It would be wonderful if they could simply renounce these habits and decide to respond to conflict in a gracious and constructive way. But it is not that easy. In order to break free from the pattern they have fallen into, they need to understand *why* they react to conflict the way they do.

Jesus provides us with clear guidance on this issue. During His earthly ministry, a young man approached the Lord and asked Him to settle an inheritance dispute with his brother. "Jesus replied, 'Man, who appointed me a judge or an arbiter between you?' Then he said to them, 'Watch out! Be on your guard against all kinds of greed; a man's life does not consist in the abundance of his possessions'" (Luke 12:13-15).

This passage reveals a common human pattern. When faced with conflict, we tend to focus passionately on what our opponent has done wrong or should do to make things right. In contrast, God always calls us to focus on what is going on in our own hearts when we are at odds with others. Why? Because our heart is the wellspring of all our thoughts, words, and actions, and therefore the source of our conflicts. "For out of the heart come evil thoughts, murder, adultery, sexual immorality, theft, false testimony, slander" (Matthew 15:19).

The heart's central role in conflict is vividly described in James 4:1-3. If you understand this passage, you will have found a key to preventing and resolving conflict.

> What causes fights and quarrels among you? Don't they come from your desires that battle within you? You want something but don't get it. You kill and covet, but you cannot have what you want. You quarrel and fight. You do not have, because you do not ask God. When you ask, you do not receive, because you ask with wrong motives, that you may spend what you get on your pleasures.

This passage describes the root cause of destructive conflict: Conflicts arise from unmet desires in our hearts. When we feel we cannot be satisfied unless we have something we want or think we need, the desire turns into a demand. If someone fails to meet that desire, we condemn him in our heart and quarrel and fight to get our way. In short, conflict arises when desires grow into demands and we judge and punish those who get in our way. Let us look at this progression one step at a time.

THE PROGRESSION OF AN IDOL[1]

I Desire

Conflict always begins with some kind of desire. Some desires are inherently wrong, such as vengeance, lust, or greed. But many desires are not wrong in and of themselves. For example, there is nothing innately wrong about desiring things like peace and quiet, a clean home, a new computer, professional success, an intimate relationship with your spouse, or respectful children.

If a good desire, such as wanting an intimate relationship with your spouse, is not being met, it is perfectly legitimate to talk about it with your spouse, as we will discuss in chapter 5. As you talk, you may discover ways that both of you can help to fulfill each other in mutually beneficial ways. If not, it may be appropriate to seek help from your pastor or a Christian counselor who can assist you in understanding your differences and strengthening your marriage (more on this in chapter 11).

But what if your spouse persistently fails to meet a particular desire and is unwilling to discuss it further with you or anyone else? This is where you stand at a crossroad. On the one hand, you can trust God and seek your fulfillment in Him (Psalm 73:25). You can ask Him to help you to continue to grow and mature no matter what your spouse does (James 1:2-4). And you can continue to love your spouse and pray for God's sanctifying work in his or her life (1 John 4:19-21; Luke 6:27-28). If you follow this course, God promises to bless you and use your difficult situation to conform you to the likeness of Christ (Romans 8:28-29).

On the other hand, you can dwell on your disappointment and allow it to control your life. At the very least, this will result in self-pity and bitterness toward your spouse. At worst, it can destroy your marriage. Let us look at how this downward spiral evolves.

I Demand

Unmet desires have the potential of working themselves deeper and deeper into our hearts. This is especially true when we come to see a desire as something we need or deserve, and therefore must have in order to be happy or fulfilled. There are many ways to justify or legitimize a desire.

▮ "I work hard all week. Don't I deserve a little peace and quiet when I come home?"

▮ "I worked two jobs to put you through school; I deserve your respect and appreciation."

▮ "I spend hours managing the family budget; I really need a new computer."

▮ "The Bible says we should save up to cover unexpected problems; we need to tighten our budget so we can put more into savings."

▮ "God has given me a gift for developing new businesses, and He calls me to work hard to support our family. I deserve to have more of your support."

▮ "Scripture says a husband and wife should be completely united in love. I need to have more intimacy with you."

▮ "I only want what God commands: children who have learned to respect their parents and use their God-given gifts to the fullest."

There is an element of validity in each of these statements. The trouble is that if our desire is not met, these attitudes can lead to a vicious cycle. The more we want something, the more we think of it as something we need and deserve. And the more we think we are entitled to it, the more convinced we are that we cannot be happy and secure without it.

When we see our object of desire as being essential to our fulfillment and well-being, it moves from being a desire to a demand. "I wish I could have this" evolves into "I must have this!" This is where trouble sets in. Even if the initial desire was not inherently wrong, it has grown so strong that it begins to control our thoughts and behavior. In biblical terms, it has become an "idol."

Most of us think of an idol as a statue of wood, stone, or metal worshiped by pagan people. But the concept is much broader and far more personal than that. An idol is anything apart from God that we depend on to be happy, fulfilled, or secure. In biblical terms it is something other than God that we set our heart on (Luke 12:29), that motivates us (1 Corinthians 4:5), that masters and rules us (Psalm 119:133; Ephesians 5:5), or that we trust, fear, or serve (Isaiah 42:17; Matthew 6:24; Luke 12:4-5). In short, it is something we love and pursue in place of God (see Philippians 3:19).

Given its controlling effect on our lives, an idol can also be referred to as a "false god" or a "functional god." As Martin Luther wrote, "To whatever we look for any good thing and for refuge in every need, that is what is meant by 'god.' To have a god is nothing else than to trust and believe in him from the heart. . . . To whatever you give your heart and entrust your being, that, I say, is really your god."[2]

Even sincere Christians struggle with idolatry. We may believe in God and say we want to serve Him only, but at times we allow other influences to rule us. In this sense we are no different from the ancient Israelites: "Even while these people were worshiping the LORD, they were serving their idols. To this day their children and grandchildren continue to do as their fathers did" (2 Kings 17:41).

It is important to emphasize the fact that idols can arise from good desires as well as wicked desires. It is often not *what* we want that is the problem, but that we want it *too much*. For example, it is not unreasonable for a man to want a passionate sexual relationship with his wife, or for a wife to want open and honest communication with her husband, or for either of them to want a steadily growing savings account. These are good desires, but if they turn into demands that must be met in order for either spouse to be satisfied and fulfilled, they result in bitterness, resentment, or self-pity that can destroy a marriage.

How can you discern when a good desire might be turning into a sinful demand? You can begin by prayerfully asking yourself "X-ray" questions that reveal the true condition of your heart.

- What am I preoccupied with? What is the first thing on my mind in the morning and the last thing on my mind at night?
- How would I complete this statement: "If only _____, then I would be happy, fulfilled, and secure"?
- What do I want to preserve or avoid?
- Where do I put my trust?
- What do I fear?
- When a certain desire is not met, do I feel frustration, anxiety, resentment, bitterness, anger, or depression?
- Is there something I desire so much that I am willing to disappoint or hurt others in order to have it?

As you search your heart for idols, you will often encounter multiple layers of concealment, disguise, and justification. As mentioned earlier, one of the most subtle cloaking devices is to argue that we want only what God Himself commands.

For example, a mother may desire that her children be respectful and obedient to her, kind to one another, and diligent in developing their gifts and talents. And she can back up each goal with a specific scripture that shows that God Himself desires such behavior.

When they do not fulfill these goals, even after her repeated encouragement or correction, she may feel frustrated, angry, or resentful. She needs to ask, "Why am I feeling this way? Is it a righteous anger that they are not living up to God's standards? Or is it a selfish anger that they are not giving me the smooth, comfortable, and convenient day I want?"

In most cases it will be a mixture of both. Part of her truly wants to see her children love and obey God in every way, both for His glory and for their good. But another part of her is motivated by a desire for her own comfort and convenience. Which desire is really controlling her heart and reactions?

If the God-centered desire is dominating the mother's heart, her response to disobedient children should be characterized by God's discipline toward her. "The LORD is compassionate and gracious, slow to anger, abounding in love" (Psalm 103:8). As she imitates God, her response will line up with corrective guidelines found in Galatians 6:1: "If someone is caught in a sin, you who are spiritual should restore him gently. But watch yourself, or you also may be tempted." In other words, although her discipline may be direct and firm, it will be wrapped in gentleness and love, and leave no residue of resentment or unforgiveness.

On the other hand, if her desire for comfort and convenience has become an idol, her reaction to her children will be much different. It will be characterized by smoldering anger as well as harsh and unnecessarily hurtful words or discipline. She may feel bitterness or resentment that her desires have been frustrated. And even after disciplining her children, she may maintain a lingering coolness toward them that extends their punishment and warns them not to cross her again. If this latter group of attitudes and actions frequently characterizes her response, it is a sign that her desire for godly children has probably evolved into an idolatrous demand.

I Judge

Another sign of idolatry is the inclination to judge other people. When they fail to satisfy our desires and live up to our expectations, we criticize and condemn in our hearts if not with our words. As Dave Powlison writes:

> We judge others—criticize, nit-pick, nag, attack, condemn—
> because we literally play God. This is heinous. [The Bible
> says] "There is only one Lawgiver and Judge, the one who is
> able to save and to destroy; but who are you to judge your
> neighbor?" Who are you when you judge? None other than a
> God wannabe. In this we become like the Devil himself (no
> surprise that the Devil is mentioned in James 3:15 and 4:7).
> We act exactly like the adversary who seeks to usurp God's
> throne and who acts as the accuser of the brethren. When
> you and I fight, our minds become filled with accusations:
> your wrongs and my rights preoccupy me. We play the self-
> righteous judge in the mini-kingdoms we establish.[3]

This insight should leave us shaking in our boots! When we judge others and condemn them in our hearts for not meeting our desires, we are imitating the Devil (see James 3:15; 4:7). We have doubled our idolatry problem: Not only have we let an idolatrous desire rule our hearts, but we have also set ourselves up as judging minigods. This is a formula for excruciating conflict.

This is not to say that it is inherently wrong to evaluate or even judge others within certain limits. As we will see in chapter 5, Scripture teaches that we should observe and evaluate others' behavior so that we can respond and minister to them in appropriate ways, which may even involve loving confrontation (see Matthew 7:1-5; 18:15; Galatians 6:1).

We cross the line, however, when we begin to sinfully judge others, which is characterized by a feeling of superiority, indignation, condemnation, bitterness, or resentment. Sinful judging often involves speculating on others' motives. Most of all, it reveals the absence of a genuine love and concern toward them. When these attitudes are present, our judging has crossed the line and we are playing God.

The closer we are to others, the more we expect of them and the more likely we are to judge them when they fail to meet our expectations. For example, we may look at our spouse and think, "If you really love me, you above all people will help meet this need." We think of our children and say, "After all I've done for you, you owe this to me."

We can place similar expectations on relatives, close friends, or members of our church. Expectations are not inherently bad. It is good to hope for the best in others and reasonable to anticipate receiving understanding and support from those who are closest to us.

But if we are not careful, these expectations can become conditions and standards that we use to judge others. Instead of giving people room for independence, disagreement, or failure, we rigidly impose our expectations on them. In effect, we expect them to give allegiance to our idols. When they refuse to do so, we condemn them in our hearts and with our words, and our conflicts with them take on a heightened intensity.

I Punish

Idols always demand sacrifices. When others fail to satisfy our demands and expectations, our idols demand that they should suffer. Whether deliberately or unconsciously, we will find ways to hurt or punish people so they will give in to our desires.

This punishment can take many forms. Sometimes we react in overt anger, lashing out with hurtful words to inflict pain on those who fail to meet our expectations. When we do so, we are essentially placing others on the altar of our idol and sacrificing them, not with a pagan knife, but with the sharp edge of our tongue. Only when they give in to our desire and give us what we want will we stop inflicting pain upon them.

But we punish those who don't bow to our idols in numerous other ways as well. Our children may use pouting, stomping, or dirty looks to hurt us for not meeting their desires. Adults and children alike may impose guilt or shame on others by walking around with pained or crushed looks on their faces. Some people even resort to physical violence or sexual abuse to punish and control others.

As we grow in faith and awareness of our sin, most of us recognize and reject overt and obviously sinful means of punishing others. But our idols do not give up their influence easily, and they often lead us to develop more subtle means of punishing those who do not serve them.

Withdrawal from a relationship is a common way to hurt others. This may include a subtle coolness toward the other person, withholding affection or physical contact, being sad or gloomy, refusing to look someone in the eye, or even abandoning the relationship altogether.

Sending subtle, unpleasant cues over a long period of time is an age-old method of inflicting punishment. For example, a friend of mine mentioned to me that his wife was not pleased with the fact that he was giving so much time to a particular ministry. He closed by saying, "And as we all know, when momma ain't happy, ain't nobody happy!" He laughed as he said it, but his comment made me think of the proverb, "A quarrelsome wife is like a constant dripping on a rainy day" (Proverbs 27:15). A woman has a unique ability to set the tone in a home. If she is not careful, she can pervert that gift and use it to create an unpleasant or uncomfortable atmosphere that tells her family, "Either get in line with what I want, or you will suffer." Such behavior is an act of unbelief: Instead of relying on God's means of grace to sanctify her family, she depends on her own tools of punishment to manipulate them into change. Of course a man can do the same thing; by being perpetually critical and unhappy, he too can make everyone in the family miserable until they give in to his idols. The usual result of such behavior is a superficial, splintered family.

Inflicting pain on others is one of the surest signs that an idol is ruling our hearts (see James 4:1-3). When we catch ourselves punishing others in any way, whether deliberately and overtly or unconsciously and subtly, it is a warning that something other than God is ruling our hearts.

REVISITING STEVE AND JULIE

Now that we understand the progression of an idol, we can look beyond the surface issues that Steve and Julie have been fighting over. We can go to the heart of their conflict.

Steve's major idol was a familiar one—his work. Success at the office demanded long hours and few vacations, and he embraced it with a passion. He loved it so much that even when he was with his family he was distant, offering only half his mind, if that, and only one ear to his wife and kids.

The making of Steve's idol started where all sins do: in the realm of desire. In his case, it was in a good desire for success in his vocation. Such success, Steve believed, was essential to his happiness and fulfillment. It was, in his own mind, something he *needed* (and *deserved*), and he had no problem justifying it—the Bible says a great deal about the virtues of hard work and providing for one's family.

Steve's desire for professional success was intensified by several related desires: pride, a longing for his father's approval, and a yearning for financial security. Together, these desires evolved into a controlling demand, unspoken to be sure, but delivered through his every action around his family: "For me to be happy and secure, and for us to work as a family, my job has to have priority over everything else." Had Steve at that point "X-rayed" his heart, asking the questions we presented earlier on page 19, he would have recognized that his work had become an idol, for his work preoccupied him, was always on his mind, and was where he placed all his trust for fulfillment and security.

Because his job was vitally important to him, Steve expected Julie to make it a top priority as well, deferring to his work demands and keeping the kids out of his hair. But she did not want to worship his idol. She was too busy serving her own idol, as we will discuss below. As a result, Steve constantly judged her for "deficiencies," which threw his marriage into constant and often excruciating conflict.

Sometimes he meted out punishment in aggressive dollops—shouted put-downs before he stormed out the door. But most of the time it was administered via emotional distance. If Julie refused to prostrate herself before *his* god, he would strip from her the intimacy he knew she wanted in their marriage.

Julie sang the same song but a different verse. She resented Steve's preoccupation with his work, but she had fallen into a trap of her own. Julie's world revolved around her children, around their schoolwork, their many extracurricular activities, and the development of their faith. She saw the kids as her province—albeit grudgingly so on occasion—and invested herself totally in their successes and failures. If the kids had a good day, living up to her expectations, Julie had a good day. If the kids had a bad day, dropping below her dreams for them or bickering with each other or seeming uninterested in the Lord, Julie became fearful and irritable. When Steve came home, she often unloaded her fears and frustrations on him, and the cycle of conflict began all over again.

Like Steve, Julie had elevated good desires to sinful demands. Nothing she wanted for her children, and herself, was wrong per se. But when she allowed these desires to preoccupy and rule her, they became her functional gods, the things she felt she needed in order to have a happy marriage and a happy and fulfilling life. When Steve didn't get with her program and worship her idols and work toward her happiness on her terms, *he* became the problem.

She judged him a poor husband and a lousy father, and she made him pay by confronting him with a sharp tongue and continual nagging. And when that did not force him to change, she pulled away from him and hid behind a coolness that discouraged any kind of meaningful intimacy.

With the idols unveiled, the conflict between Steve and Julie becomes understandable. But to understand a problem is not to solve it. What can these two Christians do to overcome their idols and bring harmony back into their marriage?

THE CURE FOR AN IDOLATROUS HEART

An idol, as we have seen, is any desire that has grown into a consuming demand that rules our heart; it is something we think we must have to be happy, fulfilled, or secure. To put it another way, it is something we love, fear, or trust.

Love, fear, trust—these are words of worship! Jesus commands us to love God, fear God, and trust God and God alone (Matthew 22:37; Luke 12:4-5; John 14:1). Any time we long for something apart from God, fear something more than God, or trust in something other than God to make us happy, fulfilled, or secure, we are engaging in the worship of false gods. As a result, we deserve the judgment and wrath of the true God.

Deliverance from Judgment

There is only one way out of this bondage and judgment: *It is to look to God Himself, who loves to deliver people from their idols.* "I am the LORD your God, who brought you out of Egypt, out of the land of slavery. You shall have no other gods before me" (Exodus 20:2-3).

God has provided the cure for our idolatry by sending His Son to experience the punishment that we deserve because of our sin. Through Jesus Christ we can become righteous in God's sight and find freedom from sin and idolatry. "Therefore, there is now no condemnation for those who are in Christ Jesus, because through Christ Jesus the law of the Spirit of life set me free from the law of sin and death" (Romans 8:1-2).

To receive this forgiveness and freedom, we must acknowledge our sin, repent of it, and put our trust in Jesus Christ (see Acts 3:19; Psalm 32:5). When we do, we are no longer under God's judgment. Instead, He brings us into His family, makes us His children and heirs, and enables us to live a godly life (Galatians 4:4-7). This is the good news of the gospel—forgiveness and eternal life through our Lord Jesus Christ!

Deliverance from Specific Idols

Yet there is more good news. God wants to deliver us not only from our general problem with sin and idolatry, but also from the specific, day-to-day idols that consume us, control us, and cause conflict with those around us.

This deliverance is not done in blanket fashion, with all our idols being swept away in one great spiritual experience. Instead, God calls us to identify and confess our idols one by one, and then to cooperate with Him as He steadily removes them bit by bit from our hearts.

God conveys His grace to help us in this identification and deliverance process via three vehicles: His Bible, His Spirit, and His church. The Bible is "living and active. Sharper than any double-edged sword, it penetrates even to dividing soul and spirit, joints and marrow; it judges the thoughts and attitudes of the heart" (Hebrews 4:12). As you diligently study and meditate on the Bible and sit under regular, sound preaching, God will use His Word like a spotlight and a scalpel in your heart. It will reveal your idolatrous desires and show you how to love and worship God with all your heart, mind, soul, and strength.

The Holy Spirit aids our deliverance from idols by helping us to understand the Bible, to identify our sin, and to pursue a godly life (1 Corinthians 2:10-15; Philippians 2:13). Therefore, we should pray on a daily basis for the Spirit to guide, convict, and strengthen us in our walk with Christ.

Finally, God has surrounded us with brothers and sisters in Christ who can teach us, lovingly confront us about our idols, and provide encouragement and guidance in our spiritual growth (Galatians 6:1; Romans 15:14). This requires that we commit ourselves to consistent involvement in a solid, biblical church and seek regular fellowship and accountability from spiritually mature believers.

Through these three vehicles of grace, God will help you examine your life and progressively expose and deliver you from the idols that rule your heart. This process involves several key steps.

- Prayerfully ask yourself the questions on page 30, which will help you discern the desires that have come to rule your heart.
- Keep track of your discoveries in a journal so that you can identify patterns and steadily go after specific idols.
- Pray daily that God would rob your idols of their influence in your life by making you miserable whenever you give in to them.
- Describe your idols to your spouse and an accountability partner, and ask them to pray for you and lovingly confront you when they see signs that the idol is still controlling you.
- Realize that idols are masters of change and disguise. As soon as you gain a victory over a particular sinful desire, your idol is likely to reappear in a related form, with a redirected desire and more subtle means of attracting your attention.
- If you are dealing with an idol that is difficult to identify or conquer, go to your pastor or some other spiritually mature advisor, and seek his or her counsel and support.
- Most of all, ask God to replace your idols with a growing love for Him and a consuming desire to worship Him and Him alone (more on this below).

If someone told you that you had a deadly cancer that would take your life if you did not get treatment, you would probably spare no effort or expense in pursuing the most rigorous treatment available. Well, you do have cancer, a cancer of the soul. It is called sin and idolatry. But there is a cure. It is called the gospel of Jesus Christ, and it is administered through the Word, the Spirit, and the church. The more rigorously you avail yourself of these means of grace, the greater effect they will have in delivering you from the idols that plague your soul.

Replace Idol Worship with Worship of the True God

In his excellent book *Future Grace,* John Piper teaches that "sin is what you do when you are not fully satisfied in God."[4] The same may be said about idolatry: It is what we do when we are not fully satisfied in God. In other words, if we are not fulfilled and secure in God, we will inevitably seek other sources of happiness and security.

Therefore, if you want to squeeze the idols out of your heart and leave no room for them to return, make it your top priority to aggressively pursue an all-consuming worship for the living God. Ask Him to teach you how to love, fear, and trust Him more than anything in this world. Replacing idol worship with worship of the true God involves several steps:

- *Repent before God.* When we repent and confess our sins and idols, believing in our forgiveness through Christ, we also confess our faith in Christ. Repentance and confession of our faith in the true God *is* true worship (1 John 1:8-10). "The sacrifices of God are a broken spirit; a broken and contrite heart, O God, you will not despise" (Psalm 51:17; see also Isaiah 66:2b).

- *Fear God.* Stand in awe of the true God when you are tempted to fear others or are afraid of losing something precious. "The fear of the LORD is the beginning of [all wisdom]" (Proverbs 1:7). "Do not be afraid of those who kill the body but cannot kill the soul. Rather, be afraid of the One who can destroy both soul and body in hell" (Matthew 10:28). "If you, O LORD, kept a record of sins, O Lord, who could stand? But with you there is forgiveness; therefore you are feared" (Psalm 130:3-4).

- *Love God.* Desire the One who forgives us and provides everything we need instead of looking to other things that cannot save you. "Jesus replied: 'Love the Lord your God with all your heart and with all your soul and with all your mind'" (Matthew 22:37). "Those who seek the LORD lack no good thing" (Psalm 34:10). "Seek first his kingdom and his righteousness, and all these things will be given to you as well" (Matthew 6:33). "Whom have I in heaven but you? And earth has nothing I desire besides you. My flesh and my heart may fail, but God is the strength of my heart and my portion forever" (Psalm 73:25-26).

- *Trust God.* Rely on the One who sacrificed His Son for you and has proven Himself to be absolutely dependable in every situation. "It is better to take refuge in the LORD than to trust in man" (Psalm 118:8). "Trust in the LORD with all your heart and lean not on your own understanding" (Proverbs 3:5). "His divine power has given us everything we need for life and godliness through our knowledge of him who called us by his own glory and goodness. Through these he has given us his very great and precious promises, so that through them you may participate in the divine nature and escape the corruption in the world caused by evil desires" (2 Peter 1:3-4).

■ *Delight in God.* Find your greatest joy in thinking about God, meditating on His works, talking to others about Him, praising Him, and giving Him thanks. "Delight yourself in the LORD and he will give you the desires of your heart" (Psalm 37:4). "My mouth is filled with your praise, declaring your splendor all day long" (Psalm 71:8). "Rejoice in the Lord always. I will say it again: Rejoice!" (Philippians 4:4). "Be joyful always; pray continually; give thanks in all circumstances, for this is God's will for you in Christ Jesus" (1 Thessalonians 5:16-18).

As these passages indicate, God has designed a wonderful cycle for those who want to worship Him above all things. As you love, praise, give thanks, and delight yourself in God, He will fulfill your desires with the best thing in the world: more of Himself! And as you learn to delight more and more in Him, you will feel less need to find happiness, fulfillment, and security in the things of this world. By God's grace, the influence of idolatry and conflict in your family can be steadily diminished, and you and your family can enjoy the intimacy and security that come from worshiping the one true God.

AS YOU GROW

1. When you are in conflict with a family member, what desires do you have that you feel are not being met?

2. In order to identify desires that may have turned into demands, ask yourself these questions:
   - What am I preoccupied with? (What is the first thing on my mind in the morning, and the last thing at night?)
   - How would I complete this statement: "If only _____, then I would be happy, fulfilled, and secure"?
   - What do I want to preserve or avoid?
   - Where do I put my trust?
   - What do I fear?
   - When a certain desire is not met, do I feel frustration, anxiety, resentment, bitterness, anger, or depression?
   - Is there something I desire so much that I am willing to disappoint or hurt others in order to have it?

3. How are you judging those who do not meet your desires? Are you feeling indignation, condemnation, bitterness, resentment, or anger?

4. How are you punishing those who do not meet your desires?

5. How can you cultivate a more passionate love for and worship of God?

DIGGING DEEPER

For more guidance on identifying and overcoming the idolatrous desires that can rule our lives, see:

▍ *Idols of the Heart*, by Elyse Fitzpatrick
▍ *When People Are Big and God Is Small,* by Ed Welch
▍ *Addictions: A Banquet in the Grave,* by Ed Welch
▍ *Future Grace,* by John Piper

3

A Biblical Framework for Peacemaking

Conflict is by no means a new thing. It goes back a long way—to the Garden of Eden. The first conflict of history, Adam and Eve versus God, had profound implications. It threw our original parents and their children into a lifetime of conflict with one another. Worse yet, it separated them from the God with whom they had originally enjoyed an intimate, personal relationship.

Unfortunately, their corruption is our corruption. Adam and Eve's sin has affected the entire human race. It is with us to this day, rearing its ugly head in our lives on a daily basis, from our first breath on this planet to our last. It's in our blood, so to speak; in our human nature, we are sinners through and through. This is why conflict is inevitable, even in the lives of God's people.

But God has not forsaken us to our sin and conflict. Because of His love for us, He sent His Son to earth to deliver us from our sin and save us from its eternal consequences (John 3:16). By taking our sins to the cross, Jesus paid for our wrongs and reconciled us with our heavenly Father (1 Peter 3:18). We are still sinners, true—the effects of the original sin remain with us—but we who trust in Christ as our Savior are saints as well (Colossians 3:12).

Christ's death on the cross dramatically changed our eternal itinerary—through faith in His completed work, we will go to heaven, not hell. But His sacrifice also opened the way for us to handle problems on earth differently. By His grace, we can confess our sins, look to God for help in healing broken relationships, and ask Him to help us change harmful attitudes and habits (1 John 1:9). It is God's grace that animates our daily lives. It is God's grace that makes a life pleasing to God possible (Philippians 2:13). And it is God's grace that allows us to resolve conflicts in a way that pleases Him and preserves precious relationships. The more we rely on His grace, the more effective we can be in living for God's glory as sinners who are also saints.

God's grace offers indescribable hope to those mired in conflict. Once we confess them, our past sins become just that—past. God is a redeeming God who *wants* to forgive our sins and does so, wiping our slate clean. God delights in turning ashes into beauty and conflict into peace, and He is always willing to help us change our ways so that we cooperate more and more with His wonderful design for our lives (2 Peter 1:3-4).

God wants His love for us to be reflected in our love for one another (John 13:34-35). Therefore, He wants us to resolve our conflicts with one another in a way that blesses those around us and strengthens our relationships (John 17:23). But He does not merely tell us that we *should* make peace with each other. He also graciously provides us with thorough instructions on *how* to resolve conflict. On top of this, He promises to guide and support us as we put these principles into practice. These divine commands and promises form the foundation for the peacemaking model we will study throughout this book.

CONFLICT PROVIDES OPPORTUNITIES

To a spouse who likes to escape from conflict, conflict is usually nothing more than an inconvenience, something to be rid of. To one intent on attacking, it is a chance for selfish gain. But to a Christian who wants to resolve a conflict through peacemaking, conflict is much, much more. It is an opportunity to draw attention to the presence and power of God.

This is essentially what the apostle Paul told the troubled group of

Christians in Corinth when they struggled under religious, dietary, legal, and family disputes.

> So whether you eat or drink or whatever you do, do it all for the glory of God. Do not cause anyone to stumble, whether Jews, Greeks or the church of God—even as I try to please everybody in every way. For I am not seeking my own good but the good of many, so that they may be saved. Follow my example, as I follow the example of Christ. (1 Corinthians 10:31-11:1)

As this passage shows, Paul viewed conflict as an opportunity to glorify God, to serve other people, and to grow to be like Christ. In today's self-absorbed world, this perspective sounds radical—or even naive and foolish. But this approach to conflict can be highly effective, and it is certainly God-pleasing.

Glorifying God is the highest calling of a Christian. When we are in the midst of conflict, we have the opportunity to give testimony to what Jesus has done for us, and to reflect the love and kindness of Christ in how we treat those who have wronged us. The more Jesus' grace and character are revealed in us, the more God is honored and praised (1 Peter 2:12).

Conflict also provides an opportunity to serve our neighbor. We are to love our neighbors as ourselves, even if they are disappointing or mistreating us (Luke 6:27-28). This is especially true with our spouse or children. When we are in a conflict, we can bless them by carrying their burdens, providing them with a positive example, confronting them in a loving and constructive way, and forgiving them as God has forgiven us (Ephesians 4:32). Such service blesses those around us and honors God.

As for growing to be like Christ, conflict is one of the many tools God can use to make us more like His Son (Romans 8:28-29). Whether it's reminding us of our weaknesses or allowing us to practice love and forgiveness in the face of provocation and frustration, conflict affords us a great opportunity to strengthen and refine our character.

These three opportunities give rise to a four-point conflict resolution system we call the "Four G's," which provide the framework for this entire book. We will present a brief overview of these four principles here, and then discuss each of them in more detail in later chapters.

Glorify God

Our God is a great and holy God, and our greatest privilege in life is to bring Him glory. One of the most significant ways we can bring honor and praise to God is by continually remembering what He did for us in His Son Jesus. The death of the God-man on the cross stands for all time as the epitome of grace and mercy; it is literally our salvation from never-ending torment in hell. When we make Christ's work on the cross the central aspect of our lives, even when involved in conflict, our lives take on a God-pleasing aroma.

In addition to being the key to the Christian life, recalling our roots in Christ is the key to glorifying God through conflict as well. Remembering what Christ has done for us inspires us to trust God, and not ourselves, for the results to any conflict we might be in (2 Peter 1:3-4). It motivates us to obey His commands (John 14:15). And it empowers us to imitate the character of Christ as we interact with those around us (Ephesians 5:1). Trusting, obeying, and imitating Christ are essential to responding to conflict in a God-pleasing manner. When we live like this, we glorify our gracious and loving God.

Trusting, obeying, and imitating God through conflict yields other benefits as well. To begin with, it sets our mind on godly things. When we think about our relationship with our loving Father, we will find it easier to resist sinful urges (pride, control, bitterness, etc.) and to respond in love and obedience to God. Our emotions—which can often be our own worst enemy—are brought under control when we focus on trusting, obeying, and imitating God, and we will be less inclined to yield to them.

Second, we will be less dependent on results and other people's behavior. Although our spouse may respond negatively, or not at all, to our peacemaking efforts, we can be content and at peace in the knowledge that we trusted and obeyed God and can thus persevere even through the most difficult circumstances.

Practically speaking, we can focus our eyes on Jesus by asking ourselves one central question during any sort of conflict: How can I please and honor God in this situation? This was the supreme thought on Jesus' mind during His earthly ministry (John 5:30; 8:29), and it should be on ours as well, especially when we are involved in conflict.

Get the Log Out of Your Own Eye

Rarely, if ever, are we wholly innocent of wrongdoing in any conflict we are involved in. Thus, our second focus in any conflict, after focusing on God, is on ourselves—not to justify our actions or develop a plan to "win" the conflict, but to examine and confess our own wrongs in the situation. This is not a natural response to conflict. Typically we will attack others and focus on their wrongs. But Jesus commands us to take a radically different approach. In Matthew 7:5, He says: "You hypocrite, first take the plank out of your own eye, and then you will see clearly to remove the speck from your brother's eye."

If we deal with conflict in this way, God will graciously help us to recognize our weaknesses and encourage us to depend more on His grace, wisdom, and power. He will also use conflict to expose and change sinful habits and attitudes in our lives. Prominent among these habits and attitudes are our penchant for putting on appearances, our stubborn pride, our unwillingness to forgive, and our critical tongue. Conflict has a way of bringing these sins to the surface, giving us the opportunity to confess them to our forgiving God.

Getting the log out of our own eye can also accelerate the resolution of a conflict. First, it allows us to more quickly face up to our contribution to a dispute. If a conflict is of our making, we can do much to resolve it simply by confessing our role and asking for forgiveness.

Second, even in conflicts where we do not believe ourselves to be the primary instigator, we have probably still played some role in exacerbating the problem. It will be difficult, if not impossible, to get our spouse to deal with his or her part in a conflict unless we take responsibility for what we have done.

And third, confessing our own wrongs—and taking pains to correct our subsequent behavior—may have a softening effect on our opponent. It may encourage our spouse to listen to us more openly and even follow our example in facing up to his or her own contribution to the problem.

The logs that we need to confess (called "planks" in some translations of the Bible) are of three basic types. The first log involves our words. Among them are hurtful words we blurt out that feed the conflict rather than starve it; sarcasm that is intended to wound others; grumbling or complaining that irritates or depresses our spouse; lies or exaggerations of the truth to strengthen our position; and gossip.

Our actions also play a role in heightening conflict. These include sins of commission or omission: laziness or negligence of our duties to our spouse, unloving criticism, failing to keep commitments, resisting godly advice, or withholding mercy and forgiveness.

The third log has to do with attitudes and motivations, especially those that are critical, negative, selfish, or oversensitive, which frequently stoke the flames of a conflict.

Removing these logs involves more than mere confession (as we will see in chapter 4). We must also change the way we think. Once we realize that our actions, attitudes, or words have been wrong, we must renounce our sin and turn to God. Depending on God to forgive us and change us—remembering always Jesus' wonderful work of salvation on the cross—will inspire and empower us to change the attitudes and habits that feed conflict.

This is difficult, but we take heart in the fact that God does not command us to do impossible things. Indeed, He always offers the grace and guidance for us to do what He wants. (We will say more about this in the next chapter.)

Getting the log out of our own eye will always bring us closer to our Lord and Savior and make us more useful instruments in His hands (1 John 1:9). And in many cases, it will also open the door with our spouse or children, enabling us to restore peace and work together to find mutually satisfactory solutions to our differences.

Go and Show Your Brother His Fault

Having removed the log from our own eye, we may move to the next step in peacemaking: showing our brother his fault. Confrontation is viewed with mixed reactions in our society. Some people love the opportunity to get in an opponent's face and talk about something they are really interested in—*his* or *her* shortcomings. Others slink away from the confrontation entirely, either because they fear it or because they have bought into our society's hedonistic, relativistic view that places a premium on letting people do their own thing, regardless of how sinful that "thing" is.

Neither response is proper, nor is either biblical. The truth is, confronting our neighbors about their sin, in a loving and constructive manner, provides us the opportunity to serve them in a number of ways.

First, sometimes God can use us to help our spouse find a better way to solve a problem than he or she would have come up with by himself or herself. In fact, if we can learn to work together, our collective efforts can often result in a much better solution than either could have achieved alone.

Second, if you approach your spouse in a loving and gracious way, God may use you to identify and lift a burden in his or her life. Frequently in families and close friendships, conflicts have less to do with actual issues and more to do with unresolved problems in the other's life. The lashing out he or she does is often a symptom of those deeper problems. Instead of harshly confronting—matching outburst for outburst or getting defensive—we can look for ways to help the others lift the burdens that are beyond their ability to carry.

Third, God can use us to assist others in discovering their own complicity in a conflict and how they can change to avoid similar problems in the future. This, in turn, can lead to repentance in their hearts and a closer walk with the Lord. Both Jesus and Paul talk about the importance of this concept (Matthew 18:15; Galatians 6:1).

Finally, loving confrontation can serve as a positive example to others. Whether you realize it or not, people are constantly watching how you handle adversity and treat those who wrong you. How you comport yourself gives others a chance to either mock Christians and reject Christ or become open to hearing the gospel. Christians watching your behavior, on the other hand, will either feel justified in responding improperly to conflict or be encouraged to honor God in their own reactions as well. Because imitation is a form of love, this last point has tremendous spillover effect with children. Kids study how their parents react to conflict, and will often imitate them when conflict arises in their lives as well.

Before we confront others, we should always consider overlooking the offense (Proverbs 19:11). Most potential conflicts can be smothered before they alight simply by covering an offense over in love and letting it go (1 Peter 4:8). Generally, an offense is minor enough to be passed over if it has not seriously dishonored God, has not permanently damaged a relationship, has not hurt other people, and is not hurting the offender himself. These criteria require elaboration, of course, and we will provide that in chapter 5.

If an offense does not pass these guidelines, then it is too serious to overlook and must be dealt with. Proper confrontation entails speaking only to build others up. Words are extremely powerful weapons, and how we use them can make or break any attempt to resolve a conflict.

Good listening skills are also key, both to understanding the problem on a practical level and to communicating positive traits to your partner, such as humility, sincerity, and genuine love and concern.

The third key to effective confrontation involves "game-planning" the encounter between you and your spouse—logistical considerations for the actual face-to-face. We will deal more fully with these three components of successful confrontation in chapter 5.

Sometimes the first attempt at a private confrontation does not work, and sometimes even repeated thoughtful attempts at personal peacemaking fail. In these cases it may become appropriate to recruit friends, church leaders, and other neutral parties to enter the discussion, as we will discuss in chapter 11.

Go and Be Reconciled

Reconciliation is one of the most comforting words in the English language. Not only does it stir our hearts when we hear of a divorced or separated couple getting back together or an adult child reuniting with long-estranged parents, but the word has spiritual ramifications that in a very real sense have transformed death to life for us.

Through the death of His Son, God has reconciled us to Himself. He has shown His love for His creation in the most tangible—and painful—way possible, and will bring His errant children back to Him to live in everlasting glory and bliss. God has, in short, forgiven us our many sins, at an incalculably great price.

And how do we, His children, react to such unmerited grace? We often have trouble forgiving others, even those we say we love. We qualify our forgiveness with such evasive phrases as "Yes, I forgive you—I just don't want to be close to you again" or "I'll forgive you this one time." Praise God that He doesn't have that attitude toward us!

God makes plain in His Word that there is a direct correlation between His forgiveness of us and our forgiveness of those who wrong us. Jesus spells this out clearly in the Lord's Prayer (Matthew 6:12; Luke 11:4) and the parable of the unmerciful servant (Matthew 18:23-35; see also Colossians 3:13).

But forgiveness is not some fuzzy, sentimental concept. Nor is it a feeling. Nor is it forgetting—God does not passively *forget* our sins; He actively chooses not to *remember* them. Nor is forgiving excusing—the very fact that forgiveness is necessary indicates that somebody did something wrong and inexcusable. And forgiveness is certainly not offering temporary remission, only to store a record of the sin in our memory and then trot it out when we need it later. Instead, forgiveness is an act of the will, a conscious decision to fully and freely pardon our offender.

When we forgive another, we break down the wall that has arisen between us and open the way for a rejuvenated relationship. We set our husband, wife, son, or daughter free from the penalty of being separated from us. This is a costly act on our part, for our human nature enjoys dredging up past wrongs and flinging them back in a person's face. To truly forgive, we have to let the offending incident go.

Here are four concrete promises one must make to truly forgive another:

- I will not think about this incident.
- I will not bring up this incident again and use it against you.
- I will not talk to others about this incident.
- I will not allow this incident to stand between us or hinder our personal relationship.

In effect, you are promising not to dwell on or brood over the incident, not to allow the matter to keep you and your spouse at a distance. God models this kind of forgiveness—and we praise Him for it. We can do no less than respond to our husband or wife in an identical manner.

Regardless of how painful the offense is, by making these promises—and delivering on them—we can, with God's help, imitate the forgiveness and reconciliation God offered us on the cross. By the grace of God—and only by the grace of God—we can forgive as He has forgiven us.

■ ■ ■

Making peace in the family can be a challenging and complicated affair; it can require many steps and involve a wide variety of biblical concepts. But the four basic principles outlined in this chapter, the "Four G's," drawn directly from the Bible, provide us with a simple and yet highly effective framework for peacemaking.

What would happen if Steve and Julie, our prototypical couple from chapter 1, used this approach to conflict? Instead of looking for ways to escape from conflict or prove that he is right and Julie is wrong, Steve would look for ways to honor God and serve his wife. He would take responsibility for his contribution to their conflict, and communicate his concerns about Julie's attitudes in a gentle and constructive way.

Similarly, instead of trying to force Steve to change through harsh confrontation, Julie would trust God to be the major agent of change in her husband. She would ask God to help her change the way she has reacted to her husband, and she would share her concerns about Steve's priorities in a more thoughtful and gracious way. And both Julie and Steve would delight in the opportunity to forgive each other in a way that honors God and provides a model that their children would be blessed to follow in their own marriages.

As both of them look for ways to glorify God, serve each other, and grow to be more like Christ, they will usually find faster and more pleasant solutions to their differences. They will also experience a growing trust and intimacy in their relationship. Most of all, they will have the peace and joy that comes from giving themselves to God and allowing Him to display His wonderful grace through their lives, even in the midst of conflict.

AS YOU GROW

1. How do you usually view conflict? Do you see it as an inconvenience, a danger, or a chance to get your way? How does your view of conflict affect your response to conflict?
2. Have you ever thought of conflict as an opportunity? How would this view of conflict affect your response to conflict?
3. How can you glorify God through conflict? Be practical and specific.
4. How can you serve your family through conflict? Be practical and specific.
5. How can you grow to be more like Christ through conflict? Again, think of practical, concrete steps you can take.
6. Go on record with the Lord by writing a prayer based on the principles taught in this chapter.

DIGGING DEEPER

Chapters 1–3 of *The Peacemaker: A Biblical Guide to Resolving Personal Conflict* provide more detailed information on developing a biblical framework for resolving conflict. These chapters explain why peace is so important to our Christian witness, how to deal with lawsuits between Christians, and how understanding the sovereignty of God can radically change the way we respond to conflict.

Part 2

THE PEACEMAKING MARRIAGE

■ ■ ■

4

Confession

"Tell you what," Stan said, grabbing a dishtowel with unusual enthusiasm, "I'll help you dry these dishes, and then we can go upstairs and watch some TV."

Martha scowled and dumped a dinner plate in the rack.

"Hey," Stan continued, "great idea to send the kids over to your mother's." He gave his wife a quick sideways embrace. "Want to watch some TV after this?"

Another plate in the rack.

Stan tightened his grip on her shoulder. "Martha, come on. I said I was sorry."

She wriggled free. "Oh, really?"

"Yeah. I'm sorry." He threw a couple rapid-fire nods her way to underline his sincerity. "So, you want to watch some TV after this?"

"What for?"

"Well, to relax, that's what for. I mean, we both had a hard day. It'll be good to—"

She wheeled on him. "No. I mean, what are you sorry for?"

"Well, you know, for . . . for making you mad."

"You're sorry for making me mad."

"Right. I'm sorry about the thing . . . the thing that made you mad."

"What thing? You're sorry about some thing that just sort of showed up at the dinner table?"

"Come on, honey. You know what I'm talking about."

"No, I don't. . . . And don't 'honey' me!" Martha turned back to the sink.

"Come on, sweetheart. I said I was sorry. Now can we go watch some TV?"

"No, we can't go watch TV," she said.

"Why not?"

She tossed the washrag in the water and turned toward him again. "Because, number one, you're not really sorry. And number two, you have no idea what you've done!"

"But I said I was sorry."

She picked up the rag again and went after the inside of a coffee cup—with vigor. "What for?"

"For ... okay, for what I said."

"And what did you say?"

"Well, you know, the thing I said about"—Stan's voice got real hesitant—"the burnt roast. I mean, it wasn't really burnt. It was good. Real good! Really!"

Again the rag in the sink. Again the face-off. "I knew it! You have no idea what you said or how you hurt me. You don't know what you're apologizing for."

"What are you talking about?"

"Well, I'm certainly not talking about some comment about a burnt roast."

"What are you so mad about then?"

Martha put her palms up in front of her shoulders and went into a little-girl pantomime, mocking Steve in a singsong voice. "'Oh sure, I understand. Melissa's out in the workforce. She has more important things to worry about than dirty diapers and clogged sinks.'"

"No, no, no," Stan said. "That's not what I mean, Martha. You know that." He grabbed a plate from the rack and swiped his towel across it. "This is a stupid thing to be upset about."

"Aha! Not only are you not sorry, but you think I'm stupid for being hurt. Well, mister, if you want a gal out in the workforce, and if dirty diapers and clogged sinks are a real turnoff for you, then maybe we're going to have to rearrange who does what around this place!" Her piece said, Martha turned back to the sink.

Stan tossed the dishtowel on the counter and gently wrapped both arms around his wife's shoulders. He wormed his chin into the cleft of her neck and said softly, "Martha, I understand now that I hurt your feelings, and I'm sorry." He adopted a pleading little voice. "I'm really sorry. Okay? Okay? C'mon, sweetheart, just a little smile. Just one little smile. Please, please, pretty please."

Martha could never resist a man on bended knee, even if only figuratively so. A smile began to crack across her stoic features.

Stan noticed the smile. "Okay," he said. He furtively checked his watch. "Let's finish up here and go upstairs. The Laker game starts in three minutes."

She tossed him off her neck like a big man going up for a rebound. "I cannot *believe* you!" she screamed.

He offered her his hands in the classic penitential pose. "Wha-a-a-a?"

"That's why you wanted to apologize."

"What are you talking about?"

"You wanted to get everything squared away before your basketball game so you wouldn't be interrupted."

"No."

"You're not sorry. You … I cannot *believe* you."

Stan adopted a come-let-us-reason-together voice. "Look, this whole thing is getting bent way out of proportion. Okay, we had the Mitchums over for dinner, right? Okay, I may have said a few things that ticked you off. But I said I'm sorry. Now can we just get things back to normal here? I mean, I did apologize and— Where are you going?"

Martha had slam-dunked the dishrag in the sink and was stomping toward the stairs. "I'm going to bed."

"Now, Martha, come on." He was immediately on her heels. "Can't we talk about it? Please, Martha…" And then under his breath he mumbled, "Now I'm never gonna see that Lakers game."

▮ ▮ ▮

Aside from the obvious lessons this story teaches about time-honored gender differences—guys will forever be a little clueless, women a little inscrutable—it communicates how difficult confession can be. Stan knew he had somehow hurt Martha's feelings during the dinner conversation with the Mitchums. But rather than deal seriously and thoroughly with his wrong, he wanted to blow it off through a superficial confession and get to what was really important for him—watching the basketball game in peace. Even when backed into a corner, he continued to offer lame, evasive words of pseudo-apology, thinking he could make up in quantity what his "apology" lacked in quality.

Martha, meanwhile, wanted the satisfaction of her husband sincerely owning up to his insensitive words. She wanted a specific confession that acknowledged exactly how he had hurt her. Needless to say, neither met their objectives that evening, and the wound opened at the dinner table was allowed to fester for at least another day.

Like Stan in this story, most of us do not like to admit that we have sinned. It rubs against our human nature. So we try to conceal, deny, or rationalize our wrongs. Failing that, we attempt to minimize them by calling them "mistakes" or "errors in judgment." If all else fails, we attempt to shift the blame or say somebody else made us do it.

Another tactic to wriggle free of confession is to use what I call the "60/40 Rule." The way this works is, I will admit to being imperfect, and thus am probably at least somewhat to blame for the problem. Let's say 40 percent of the problem is mine. That means 60 percent of the problem is my partner's. So, based on those numbers, which one of us should confess first? It is almost always the other person.

These are all foolish ways to approach confession. None would meet with God's approval. He explains explicitly in His Word that none of us is without sin, and that when we claim that we are totally innocent we only deceive ourselves (1 John 1:8). We cannot deny, conceal, excuse, rationalize, or minimize our sins when we approach our God. But thankfully, we can rest secure in the assurance that when we do confess our sins before Him, He promises to forgive them. As Proverbs 28:13 promises, "He who conceals his sins does not prosper, but whoever confesses and renounces them finds mercy."

It is this principle, that confession leads to forgiveness, which governs the whole peacemaking process. It is certainly the operating principle that restores peace between us and our God. And for effective peacemaking efforts here on earth, it should be the primary engine that motivates conflict resolution within families.

IT TAKES TWO TO TANGLE

Puffed up with self-absorption, living in a world where asserting one's rights is considered one of the, if not *the*, most important aspects of our lives, it is not easy to confess one's contribution to a conflict. But the fact is, we frequently contribute in some way to relational problems. Whether it be through our words, our thoughts, our motives, our attitudes, or our deeds, we are more often than not guilty of either starting or at least aggravating any conflict we are involved in.

Therefore, the first step in making peace with a spouse is almost always confession. To confess our sins, we must first examine ourselves, considering how our thoughts and conduct have contributed to the problem.

The best place to start this self-examination process is by thinking about our *words*. What have we been saying to or about our spouse? Words are powerful instruments, capable of great good or great harm. When used destructively, they are often the spark that sets the forest of conflict ablaze.

Have you, when faced with disagreement or offense, blurted out hurtful words that feed the conflict rather than starve it?

Are you frequently grumbling or complaining? This can have a profound effect on your partner. It creates a negative atmosphere for day-to-day family life, and in addition to irritating or depressing your spouse, it can also indirectly encourage grumbling and complaining in him or her.

How about telling lies to strengthen your position in the conflict? These "lies" don't have to be outright falsehoods, either. Often we tell only part of the truth, or we exaggerate or emphasize only the facts favorable to our argument, thus distorting the truth. Any time we distort the truth, we are guilty of lying.

Or gossiping? To gossip means to discuss personal facts about others with someone who is not part of the problem or its solution. Have you betrayed your marital confidence by bad-mouthing your spouse to others? How about to the guys around the coffee machine at work? Or even worse: Have you slandered your spouse to either make yourself feel better or gain a tactical advantage in the conflict? False and malicious talk is repeatedly forbidden in Scripture (see, for example, Leviticus 19:16; Titus 2:3).

If your self-examination yields no sinful speech, then examine your *actions*. Have you committed any sins of commission or omission in the conflict, and thus made it worse rather than better? Has your temper gotten the better of you on occasion? Have you been lazy or negligent in your duties to the other person? Have you resisted godly advice or withheld mercy and forgiveness?

Perhaps failure to heed your responsibilities has started or contributed to your conflict. Did you make a commitment you did not keep? A great deal of family conflict derives from spouses or children failing to make good on a promise or commitment.

Rebellion against or misuse of authority is also a prime source of conflict, both within and outside of the family. Have you as a husband misused your authority over your family, failing to yield to the headship of Christ in all family matters? Or conversely, have you as a wife failed to show your submission to your Lord through your submission to your husband? We must remember that when we rebel against properly established authority, we rebel against God Himself (Romans 13:2).

A succinct—and unfailingly effective—way to examine yourself is by applying the Golden Rule to your actions. How happy would you be if your spouse treated you the way you are treating him or her in this situation?

This brings us to the third and most important area of self-examination: our *attitudes and motivations*. Often we contribute to conflict with critical, negative, or overly sensitive attitudes that cause unnecessary offense or aggravate otherwise manageable differences. In Philippians 4:2-9, the apostle Paul provides us with an "attitude checkup," which describes how Christians should think when faced with conflict. Meditating on this passage can help you to identify attitudes that need to be confessed and renounced.

Even more importantly, we must relentlessly identify any idols that may be governing our words and actions. As we saw in chapter 2, these desires-raised-to-demands can range from the obviously negative (quest for control or power, greed, etc.) to the seemingly positive (such as a desire for peace and quiet, intimacy, professional success, or obedient children). Whatever they may be, any of these desires can grow so strong that they rule our hearts and lead us to judge and punish those who deny us what we want. These idols must be identified, confessed, and renounced if we want to restore peace in our relationships.

THE SEVEN A'S OF CONFESSION

After examining our words, actions, and attitudes and motivations, we must actually confess our sins. But as Stan illustrated at the beginning of this chapter, our confessions are often rendered meaningless, or worse yet, backfire, because we do not know how to properly admit our wrongs to one another. How often have you heard somebody say "I'm sorry if I hurt you" or "Let's just forget the past" or "I guess it's not *totally* your fault"? If you're on the receiving end of such "confessions," you may be temporarily pacified, but genuine satisfaction will elude you.

Thankfully, the Bible offers clear and specific guidelines for an effective confession. I call them the Seven A's of Confession.

1. Address Everyone Involved

Since all sins constitute rebellion against God, we should begin a confession by laying our sins—and ourselves—at His feet. This is *primary* in any proper confession. (In fact, this penitential posture before God and its attendant humble attitude is also the key to living the Christian life.) Only through reconciling with God will we have the inclination—and ability—to reconcile with our spouse or children.

Although all our sins, including our thoughts, require repentance before God, not all sins need to be confessed to other people. Many heart sins, ones that take place only in our thoughts, do not directly affect others. Thus we usually need confess them only to God. (If, however, a heart sin has an ongoing grip on us, it may be necessary to confess it to a spiritually mature friend or counselor who can help us find a way to overcome it.)

The problem is, heart sins often give rise to *social* sins, which affect and hurt others. Maybe the social sin is an action, such as gossiping, slandering, or lying. Or maybe it's something you should do but don't—you ignore your wife, you give your husband the cold shoulder, you fail to forgive. In either case, whenever your words or actions have affected someone else, they should be confessed to the person you wronged (James 5:16).

If you affected only one person, then you need only confess to that person. But if your sin affected more than one, *each* person should receive your confession. Optimally, you should do this privately, as this allows for feedback and furthers the opportunity for forgiveness. But if a group of people is involved, such as your entire family, you may make your confession to the entire group at one time.

A friend of mine had the chance to practice this principle during his first month as a pastor. During a sermon one Sunday morning, Paul began speaking of the importance of the origins of our spiritual beliefs, of where we get our theology. At one point in the sermon he told a joke on his wife, Heather, who was sitting in the front pew. Looking directly at her, he said, "Some people get their theology from people like Oprah and Rosie O'Donnell." He smiled, and the congregation had a good laugh.

Heather, however, turned fire-engine red. She was a serious student of the Bible, reading theological books to buttress her already strong foundation in God's Word. Therefore, she was profoundly embarrassed by her husband's comment.

The two had to return home from church in separate cars, but the moment Paul walked through the door he rushed to Heather, his eyes filled with tears. After taking her into his arms, he offered a full and complete confession of his actions. He knew he had embarrassed and hurt her, so he expressed genuine sorrow for his words and begged for her forgiveness.

Heather, of course, forgave him, as she knew she must. She expressed her forgiveness in words and mentally committed herself to live by it. God, after all, had forgiven her many wrongs; she could do no less to her repentant husband. They hugged, and she mentally closed the book on the incident.

Nevertheless, Heather's hurt lingered. She worried that many of the members of the congregation, not knowing her well, would believe that she actually took theological guidance from the shallow and false teaching propounded on empty TV talk shows.

Although he never mentioned it to her, Paul was sensitive to her worries. As he came to the pulpit the following Sunday, he placed his notes and Bible on the stand and had a heart-to-heart with his congregation. "During the sermon last week," he said, "I made my wife the object of some humor. The joke alluded to something untrue, and I embarrassed her and hurt her feelings. I have already expressed my sorrow to her, and she has forgiven me. However, because it was a public offense, I need to confess this also to you. As your pastor, I must model the way a husband is to love and honor his wife. I did not do that. I did not use humor in a responsible way. I will aim in the future to only use humor in appropriate ways. For all of this again, I am sorry and I ask for your forgiveness."

The congregation had never heard a pastor confess like this. They were so surprised that they sat there in silence for a few moments. Then a few women began to cry, and others began to nod their heads or smile to show that they appreciated Paul's confession. After the service, several people approached Paul to thank him for his example and to encourage him in his commitment to model and not merely talk about what the Bible teaches about peacemaking.

2. Avoid If, But, and Maybe

We've seen it more times than we care to remember: A politician approaches a bank of microphones after being found out in some suspect activity and offers us a confession full of *ifs, buts, maybes, perhapses,* and *possiblys.*

Such weasel-worded "confessions" generally don't work with the public, and they are absolute death to confession in a marriage. The reason they are used in the first place is to excuse the confessor's role in the incident—to blame others for the sin or, at the least, to minimize his or her guilt.

So, instead of saying "*Perhaps* I was wrong," be honest and drop the "perhaps." Rather than "*Maybe* I could have tried harder," forget the "maybe." Instead of "*Possibly* I should have waited to hear your side of the story," put some teeth in your confession by saying, "I was wrong not to wait to hear your side of the story."

The two little words *if* and *but* are so easy to use and so sure to destroy a confession. How galling is it—and counterproductive, too—to hear a spouse try to smooth over a conflict with "I'm sorry *if* I've done something to upset you." By adding that little qualifier "if," you are implying that you're not really sure whether you even committed an offense. Small wonder that genuine forgiveness rarely follows "if" confessions.

More destructive even than *if* is *but*, as in "I shouldn't have lost my temper, but I was tired." Or even worse: "I shouldn't have lost my temper, but sometimes you really frustrate me." Those little "but's" are powerful words: They cancel out everything that precedes them in these sentences. When people hear them, they sense that you believe the words that follow the "but" more than you do those that precede it.

Words such as these rarely lead to reconciliation; in fact, they postpone it. In essence they communicate that you have not yet taken responsibility for your actions or words, and that you are not likely to change your behavior in the future. All you want is for the conflict to be swept under the rug for now, but you'll probably do the same thing again at a later time.

Therefore, if you want to make a sincere confession, consciously avoid the use of any words that seem to minimize your responsibility or shift blame to others. If you admit your wrongs frankly and without reservation, you are far more likely to experience forgiveness and reconciliation.

3. Admit Specifically

Closely related to weasel words are vague generalities. This was Stan's problem in the illustration that kicked off this chapter. He wanted a positive response from Martha so he could watch his basketball game in peace, but he wouldn't come right out and confess to her what he had done wrong. The result was no basketball game— and no peace.

If you want to show that your confession is sincere, you should be as precise as possible. By specifically admitting what you did wrong, and even the biblical command you violated, you will communicate to your spouse that you are honestly facing up to the problem, which makes it easier for him or her to forgive you. Also, being specific helps you identify the behavior that needs to be changed.

A successful confession will address not only actions, but attitudes as well. If you can specifically identify an attitude that led to your behavior— be it pride, selfishness, ingratitude, bitterness, or self-righteousness—your partner will be encouraged to believe your repentance genuine. You have shown that you've driven to the heart of the issue and are willing to take whatever steps are necessary to correct your behavior.

For example, instead of saying, "I know I've been a lousy husband," you could say,

> I've sinned against God and you. He commands me to love
> you as Christ loves His church, giving Himself for her. I
> haven't even come close to that. Instead of loving you, I've
> pursued my own desires even when it's hurt you and the kids.
> I've been lazy and undisciplined, and I've broken commit-
> ment after commitment to you. I'm surprised you've put up
> with me as long as you have.

When a wife hears this kind of confession, she knows that something significant is taking place. She sees you beginning to recognize the root causes of your behavior and to identify the behavior that needs to change. Such a confession helps to create hope that things really will be different as the two of you work together to change your marriage.

4. Apologize

Another way to encourage a positive response to your confession is to make sure it includes an apology, making plain your sorrow for hurting your spouse's feelings or interests. The most effective apologies are those that communicate that you understand how he or she felt because of your actions or words. For example:

- "I can see why you are frustrated with me. I broke my word again, and I know this must make you feel like I don't care about you or your feelings. I am so sorry."
- "My comment about stay-at-home mothers was so wrong, and I know it hurt you deeply. I'm very sorry I said that."
- "I am so sorry for embarrassing you by telling everyone at the office what happened yesterday. You are always sensitive about my feelings, so I'm sure my thoughtlessness must be especially painful."

Describing a similar experience in your own life, and how that made you feel, is another way to make an apology meaningful. For example: "I remember when my dad broke his word to me. It hurt so much to think that his job was more important than going camping together. I know you must feel the same way, or even worse, since I've broken so many commitments to you."

However you do it, make a conscious effort to specifically acknowledge that you have hurt your spouse's feelings, and indicate your sorrow for doing so. It may still take your spouse some time to work through all of his or her feelings, but your apology should help to speed the process.

5. Accept the Consequences

Actions have consequences. If, in offering your confession, you willingly accept the consequences of your wrong, you communicate to your spouse that your confession is sincere. You are not simply attempting to smooth things over and be released from your responsibilities.

This may involve fulfilling a promise you reneged on, or it may entail approaching others who were involved in your offense and setting matters straight. For example, if you belittled your spouse to friends at a dinner party, going directly to those people and setting the record straight goes a long way in persuading your spouse that you truly are sorry for your behavior.

The more committed you are to making restitution and repairing the damage you have caused, the more likely your spouse will be to take your confession as sincere and be reconciled to you.

6. Alter Your Behavior

The Bible tells us to put our words into actions: "Dear children, let us not love with words or tongue but with actions and in truth" (1 John 3:18). Nothing gives credibility to a confession like an actual change in your behavior.

By explaining to your spouse that with God's help you will alter your behavior in the future, you demonstrate that your repentance is sincere. It may even be beneficial to ask your spouse for suggestions as to how you can change. To cement your earnestness, you may want to write down those suggestions and check back periodically with your spouse to see how you are doing.

However you determine to do it, changing behavior is difficult. But take heart in the fact that God does not command us to do impossible things. He always offers the grace and guidance for us to do what He wants, and we appropriate that grace by kneeling before Him on a daily basis, confessing our sins and asking for the strength to change.

Through prayer we can request that God develop in us what Paul calls the "fruit of the Spirit" (Galatians 5:22-23). By learning to delight more deeply in the Lord, we can replace the idols that rule our life with a greater love for and devotion to God. By diligent study of His Word we can identify and guard against the worldly motivations that fuel our destructive behavior, and we can develop and enhance the character qualities that are conducive to peace. And by using our opportunities in conflict to practice the behaviors God wants from us, we can further develop a Christlike character (Ephesians 4:24).

7. Ask for Forgiveness and Allow Time

The final step in a confession is to ask your spouse to forgive you. You cannot demand or force forgiveness. By asking for it you simply acknowledge that the other person now has a choice to make.

People react to confession in different ways. Some forgive immediately, while for others it takes more time. If your spouse is of the latter type, allow him or her the time needed to work through his or her feelings.

If your spouse's decision is delayed for an overly long time, you may want to backtrack and examine whether you have faithfully fulfilled the previous six steps of confession. If you pass this "examination," you may want to emphasize verbally to your spouse your sincerity and willingness to change your behavior. You will also want to pray for—and with—your spouse, asking God to give him or her the grace to forgive you.

If a long period of time elapses and your sincere efforts do not yield forgiveness from your spouse, you may want to enlist the help of your pastor or a trusted friend. As you do so, your goal should not be to simply find relief for yourself, but more significantly to see areas where you may still need to change, and to help your spouse deal with any barriers that are preventing him or her from experiencing the freedom of forgiveness.

■ ■ ■

Before we move on to the topic of confrontation, we should mention two important points about confession. First, not all seven steps are always necessary. Minor offenses particularly are often settled with a fairly simple statement. For more serious offenses, though, the wise spouse will want to make a thorough confession, going through all the Seven A's of Confession.

And second, be careful not to use these seven A's as a ritualistic formula. We should always see them for what they are intended to do: bring glory to God and serve other people. It is not a mere ceremony we go through to get the weight off our own shoulders, thus minimizing the severity of our sin in the process.

Focus your attention on pleasing God and ministering to your spouse. Strive sincerely to repair any damage you have caused and to change your behavior in the future. If you do this, you are on the fastest road to genuine peace and reconciliation.

AS YOU GROW

If you are presently involved in a conflict, these questions will help you to apply the principles presented in this chapter.

1. As you have talked to and about others in this situation, have you been guilty of any of the following kinds of speech? If so, describe what you said.
   a. Reckless words
   b. Grumbling and complaining
   c. Falsehood
   d. Gossip
   e. Slander
   f. Harsh or abusive speech
   g. Hurtful criticism
   h. Speculating on your spouse's motives

2. Are you guilty of any of the following sins in this situation? If so, describe what you did or failed to do.
   a. Uncontrolled anger
   b. Bitterness
   c. Vengeance
   d. Evil or malicious thoughts
   e. Sexual immorality
   f. Substance abuse
   g. Laziness
   h. Defensiveness
   i. Self-justification
   j. Stubbornness
   k. Resistance to godly advice
   l. Withholding mercy and forgiveness
   m. Breaking your word
   n. Misusing authority
   o. Rebelling against authority

3. What idols have influenced your words and behavior in this situation? (Remember, these desires may be inherently sinful, or they may be good things that have grown into demands that rule your heart.)

4. Write an outline for a confession.
    a. *Address everyone involved.* To whom do you need to confess?
    b. *Avoid if, but, and maybe.* What excuses or blaming do you need to avoid?
    c. *Admit specifically.* What sins have you committed? What biblical principles have you violated?
    d. *Apologize.* How might others feel as a result of your sin?
    e. *Accept the consequences.* What consequences do you need to accept? How can you reverse the damage you have caused?
    f. *Alter your behavior.* What changes do you intend to make, with God's help, in the way you think, speak, and behave?
    g. *Ask for forgiveness and allow time.* What might make the person whom you have wronged reluctant to forgive you? What can you do to make it easier for that person to forgive you?

5. Go on record with the Lord by writing a prayer based on the principles taught in this chapter.

DIGGING DEEPER

Chapters 4–6 of *The Peacemaker: A Biblical Guide to Resolving Personal Conflict* provide more detailed information on getting the log out of your own eye. These chapters explain how to overcome a critical attitude, how to balance rights and responsibilities, and how to identify and free yourself from sinful attitudes and habits that lead to conflict.

5

Confrontation

Larry was having a tough day at the office. The midquarter spreadsheets that had been tossed on his desk in the morning revealed that his new sales program was falling well short of projections. By 11:00 A.M. his boss was in his office demanding an explanation. Larry had to work through lunch and all afternoon digging through numbers and rallying his already-overworked sales force. His commute home was stop-and-go all the way, which only heightened his frustration.

As he drove up to his house, he noticed that his son had left his bicycle in the driveway again. By the time he got out of his car, moved the bike, and parked in the garage, his stomach had become a tight knot.

No one was in the kitchen when he walked in. He dropped his briefcase on the floor and went immediately to the day's mail, thumbing through the letters on the kitchen counter. Noticing a bill from his wife's health club, he opened it and was dismayed to see that they had raised their dues another 10 dollars.

Carol, his wife, walked in from the dining room. "Ah! You're home!" She smiled and opened her arms for a hug.

Larry wasn't in the mood. "So the health club is going to squeeze another 10 bucks out of us every month, huh?" he said.

Carol halted in mid-stride. The smile vanished, the arms went limp at her side. "As I recall, Larry, it was your idea for me to join the club," she said.

"Yeah, I was tired of hearing you go on and on about your weight. I hoped maybe you'd take it seriously and lose a few pounds. But at these prices"—he threw the bill on the kitchen table—"I wonder whether it's worth it, especially with you snacking *constantly* between meals and never passing up a piece of dessert."

Carol picked up the bill to have a look. "Like you're one to talk," she said. "At least I'm trying to lose weight. I don't see your spare tire getting any *smaller* these days. You won't even walk around the block with me."

Larry dismissed her comment with a wave of his hand and turned his attention to the rest of the mail. "It's not just the 10 bucks for the club," he continued, grabbing a department store bill and ripping it open. "It's all the other stuff you buy. It's your Liz Claiborne tastes and our Dress Barn budget. Look at this." He tossed that bill on the table. "Two hundred seventy-five bucks from Nieman Marcus last month. Boy, I'm going to have to take on another job just to keep up with you and the kids."

Now it was Carol's turn to slam a bill on the table. "If you want to talk money," she said fiercely, "maybe we should start by discussing the new golf clubs you just couldn't live without. That super-duper driver alone would finance a year's dues at the health club."

With that, they glared at each other for a moment before returning to their respective corners—she to the bedroom, he to the TV. Thus ended round one of another happy evening in the domestic lives of Larry and Carol.

■ ■ ■

Couples, including Christian couples, frequently face real issues in their married lives. For Larry it was his wife's appearance and her ability to manage the family's finances—both very sensitive issues in any marital relationship. But instead of approaching them with sensitivity, he simply blurted out his frustrations, loading them with even more emotion because of the stress of unrelated problems at the office.

Important, sensitive issues deserve airing between spouses. In fact, marital life runs much more smoothly when couples can raise important issues and work through them in a respectful, God-pleasing manner. Fortunately, the Bible provides numerous communication principles that can help us to discuss sensitive issues in a way that strengthens relationships and promotes constructive solutions to our differences.

OVERLOOK WHAT YOU CAN, WHEN YOU CAN

Before we delve into the principles of confrontation, let's talk about when they're not needed. The members of any normal family irritate and offend one another on a regular basis. If we all made an issue of every little thing, we would be doing nothing in the family setting *but* confronting one another on these little grievances.

A much better way to approach such small matters is to imitate the way God deals with us. We sin against Him continually, and yet He does not deal harshly with us over every offense we commit. "The Lord is compassionate and gracious, slow to anger, abounding in love" (Psalm 103:8). "Be merciful, just as your Father is merciful" (Luke 6:36). When we overlook the wrongs others commit against us, we are imitating God's extraordinary forgiveness.

Unfortunately, we cannot make a neat list of what actions or words constitute an "overlookable" offense, because everybody is different, and what one partner would consider a minor, inconsequential offense might deeply offend the other partner.

But we can offer two general rules. First, you should not overlook something that does lasting damage to your relationship with the other. If what your spouse does or says changes your feelings, thoughts, words, or actions toward him or her for more than a brief period of time, you must deal with it.

The second general guideline is a little more complex. It is this: You should not overlook an offense that does serious damage to God's reputation, to other people, or to the offender. For example, if your husband, a Christian, is consistently talking and acting around the house in a way that makes you and the children think less of God, the church, or the Bible, you will have to deal with this problem. Sins that obviously and significantly affect a person's Christian witness have to be confronted.

In the same vein, an offense that results in measurable harm to you or others must likewise be confronted. For example, if your wife gets angry behind the wheel, endangering her children and everyone else in the car with erratic driving habits, this problem must be dealt with.

The same rule applies to a problem that is affecting the offender himself or herself, especially if it is part of an ongoing pattern. Obvious examples of this would be one who misuses alcohol or prescription drugs. But offenses that impair the offender's relationship with God should also be dealt with seriously. In fact, as countercultural as it may seem, you are doing this person a great service by being concerned about his or her spiritual life. You are indeed serving that person.

If an offense does not cross one of these lines, it should probably be overlooked, and you should trust God to work in the person's life to bring about needed change. But if the offense is too big to overlook, you will need to prayerfully bring it to the attention of the other person in a way that will encourage repentance and change.

BUILD UP, DON'T TEAR DOWN

We've spoken frequently about the importance of words in any conflict. Although nonverbal actions communicate powerfully on their own—folding one's arms across one's chest, frowning, shaking one's head no—actual words coming out of your mouth connect much more forcefully with another person. When misused, these words can pound a wedge between husband and wife, driving them further and further apart. But when used properly, words can promote understanding and encourage agreement. As Proverbs 12:18 warns, "Reckless words pierce like a sword, but the tongue of the wise brings healing."

If you want to reduce the need for confrontation in your marriage, cultivate the habit of using your words to encourage and build up your spouse. Be diligent in thanking your spouse for what he or she does, acknowledging his or her efforts, and praising his or her accomplishments. In addition to verbalizing your love for the other, this habit also makes criticism easier to receive. If you are generally supportive and encouraging, your spouse will be less inclined to say, "All you do is criticize me," or to doubt your motives when you feel compelled to discuss a problem.

No matter how positive you are, there may still be times when you need to confront your partner. When this happens, it is crucial that you demonstrate love and humility by speaking with patience and gentleness. By approaching the other in a courteous way, verbalizing your concern for him or her, he or she will frequently be more ready to hear what you have to say.

Larry, in our opening illustration, would have had much better results had he said something like this: "Carol, I value and appreciate your handling the family's finances, but I am concerned about some of the expenses that are popping up these days. I love you and want to provide for you, but I need your help in watching our spending. Could we sit down later this evening and talk about this?" Broaching a concern with kindness and humility, making sure he verbalized his love for Carol, would have probably encouraged her to respond in a similar manner.

Occasionally, however, when the gentle approach doesn't get your spouse's attention, it may be necessary to confront him or her in a firm and direct manner. But even in these cases, it still makes sense to at least start gently. The stronger your words, the more likely your spouse is to respond with defensiveness and antagonism. And once the tone for a confrontation is set, it is hard to move it to a friendlier place.

The Bible is filled with practical communication tips. One of the best is found in Ephesians 4:29: "Do not let any unwholesome talk come out of your mouths, but only what is helpful for building others up according to their needs, that it may benefit those who listen." If you use this verse as a constant filter for your words, you will usually find your spouse far more willing to listen to what you have to say.

BE QUICK TO LISTEN

What comes out of your mouth is only one part of a successful confrontation. What goes into your ears, and how you receive it, is equally if not more important.

Unfortunately, listening is not a skill we come by naturally, especially in this visual age; it requires conscious attention and practice. But it is absolutely essential to successful confrontation. Its benefits are many. Having good listening skills allows us to gather more accurate information. It sends positive signals—that you don't have all the answers, that you value your spouse's views. It demonstrates your love and concern and shows your sincerity and good faith. And finally, it creates an atmosphere of mutual respect; it tells your spouse that you are not driving down a one-way street.

There are five listening skills that are particularly helpful when resolving conflict.

Waiting

Good things come to those who wait, it is said, and this applies as much to successful confrontation as it does to other areas of life. But waiting does not come naturally to us. You're the one with the issue, you're the one burning to say your piece, and now you have to keep your mouth shut?

It may be hard, but it is ever so important. For by waiting to hear what your spouse is saying, you get closer to the root of the problem, and equally important, you avoid throwing gas onto the conflict with hasty comments.

You can improve your waiting ability by focusing on three nonverbal responses. First, learn to be comfortable with silence. People are different in how they express themselves; some intersperse their statements with periods of silence—they think while they talk, not before. Respect that habit and refrain from vaulting yourself into a discussion. If the silence becomes lengthy and you don't know whether to speak, say something like, "May I respond to that, or would you like to say something more?"

Second, don't jump to conclusions. Even if you know where your spouse is going with his or her words, refrain from getting there before he or she does. You might miss what is really being saying.

And third, don't interrupt. This is especially hard when your spouse is saying something you wholeheartedly disagree with, but in time you'll have your say—wait for it. This also applies to offering solutions in the midst of the conversation. Some people don't want to hear your solutions while they're laying out their concerns. Some might even already *know* the solutions to their problems. What they want is your understanding, your compassion, your tenderness. By jumping in with answers to every problem that comes up, you deny your spouse these important nonverbal responses.

Attending

Our minds think four times faster than we can speak. While this is a good thing generally, it does make listening difficult. For our minds can be running all over looking for something to think about while they should be focusing on what our spouse is saying, and as a result missing much of it. In addition, your spouse can usually tell when you tune out of a conversation, and this only exacerbates the confrontation.

Thus it is crucial that you *attend* to your spouse's words. And this requires effort, deliberate and persistent concentration on what he or she is saying. No gazing out the window, no examining your cuticles, no disassembling your ballpoint pen, no checking your lipstick in your compact mirror.

But even if all your concentration is directed toward your spouse, there are still temptations. The primary one is figuring out what you're going to say next. We all do this from time to time, and when we do we likely miss what our conversation partner is actually saying. Plus, it is irritating. Reverse roles for a second: Can you usually tell when your spouse is a little too quick with a response? Well, if you can tell, so can your spouse when you do the same. Therefore, strive to consciously avoid this habit; direct full and undivided attention to what your spouse is saying.

It also helps to substantiate your complete attention with visual and verbal signs. Some visual signs: Maintain steady eye contact. Don't fold your arms, drum your fingers, tap your foot, or engage in similar negative body language. Lean forward slightly—this shows interest— and offer warm and responsive facial expressions. And nod your head in corroboration on occasion. Such actions may seem trivial, but experts say over half of what we say is communicated through such nonverbal expressions.

As for verbal expressions, an occasional "hm-m-m-m," "uh-huh," "I see," or "oh" tells your spouse that his or her words are getting through. These utterances also encourage him or her to continue talking.

Clarifying

It is important that you understand what your spouse is thinking, what he or she really means. Doing so often requires asking clarifying questions, or making statements that indicate you are trying to understand. These could include:

- ▌ "Are you saying…?"
- ▌ "Tell me more about…"
- ▌ "Can you give me an example?"
- ▌ "I'm confused about…"
- ▌ "What did you mean when you said…?"

Properly employing this listening skill will show that you are engaged in the conversation—you're listening and want to know as much as possible about your spouse's side of the story. This in turn will encourage further conversation, and the resulting dialogue may more clearly unearth underlying concerns, motives, and feelings.

Focus on *who, what, when, where, why,* and *how,* and avoid questions that can be dismissed with a simple yes or no. Also, remember the intent of these questions—they are to *clarify* matters, not to embarrass or trap your spouse.

Reflecting

Our fourth listening skill involves the use of reflecting (paraphrasing) statements. This entails simply—and briefly—summarizing what your spouse has just said and returning it to him or her in a tidy verbal package. Include both the content of what your spouse has said as well as his or her apparent feelings.

These paraphrases should be brief and to the point, and they should not divert attention away from the speaker. They should be said with an appropriate tone of voice and accompanied by suitable body language. Here are some examples:

- "You believe I didn't take time to hear you out."
- "The way you see it, then, is..."
- "You seem to believe I was being dishonest (or harsh, insensitive, etc.) about..."
- "I get the impression I've really disappointed you."
- "You were really hurt by my comment about you at the dinner table."

Note, however, that you are not necessarily agreeing with your spouse; you are simply validating his or her perceptions. You are saying you have heard them and comprehend them. After all, perceptions don't have to be true to be real, and by taking those impressions and reformulating them, you are telling your spouse that you understand how he or she feels. This is crucial for a successful confrontation, because once your spouse says, "You don't even care about how this has affected me," no number of "That's not true's" or "Yes, I do's" is going to change his or her mind. To seriously deal with the behavior that gave rise to the perceptions, you must take, and understand, the perceptions at face value.

Reflecting serves a host of positive purposes. It proves you are paying attention and reduces the need for repetition and raised voices to get points across. It clarifies your spouse's statements and focuses the discussion on a single topic rather than allowing it to wander here and there. It slows down the pace of the conversation, a beneficial by-product when emotions are running high. And by reflecting seriously and deliberately on what your spouse is saying, you encourage a similar response later on in the conversation.

Agreeing

Agree with your spouse about what you can, and agree with him or her as often as you can. Certainly you are not expected to abandon your beliefs; you are simply agreeing with what you can when you can—you'll get your chance to disagree soon enough. This fifth and often most important listening skill will encourage your spouse to open up.

One of the most productive times to agree is when you realize you have been in the wrong. A well-placed "You're right. I was wrong about what I said" or "You know, a lot of what you said is true: I do have to deal with my temper (or attitude, language, etc.)" or "I can understand why you would be upset with my being late again" can turn a potential argument into a constructive discussion.

The trouble is, agreeing with people who are pointing out your faults is not an easy task. How is it done? Resist the impulse to defend yourself, blame somebody else, or focus on points of disagreement. Ask yourself: "Is there *any* truth at all in what my spouse is saying?" Seize each opportunity to agree with him or her.

If you, like many people, are worried that by agreeing to one fault you are accepting responsibility for the entire problem, then phrase your agreement in specifics. Tell him or her exactly what you are agreeing with—that you failed to keep a commitment, you do occasionally fly off the handle, or you are sometimes home late—but also mention that you do not believe that your behavior is wholly responsible for the problem.

By agreeing with your spouse as much as you can, you are more likely to move the conversation in a positive direction and create an atmosphere where you are both seeking to understand and work toward a constructive solution. It takes work and self-discipline, but it is one of the best ways to resolve conflict and restore peace.

HEAL WITH WISE COMMUNICATION

We have looked at the crucial aspect of using only edifying words in a confrontation, not tearing your spouse down. We have also considered the importance of employing proper listening skills during the conversation. Now we come to the confrontation proper. How should it be staged, and what exactly should you say?

Logistical Considerations

The wrong setting and improper timing can destroy the effect of important occasions. For example, you probably did not ask your wife to marry you during halftime at a football game, right? So it is with a confrontation: This is a serious endeavor to which you have given much thought. If you want it to be successful, you need to plan carefully.

Here are some guidelines. First, do not engage your spouse in a serious talk when either of you is tired, in a bad mood, or preoccupied by other matters. Also, make sure you schedule a time that is open-ended—not 15 minutes before your family leaves for church or 10 minutes before your spouse leaves for work. Such an important issue deserves as much time as it needs. Do not hem it in with time constraints.

As for where the confrontation takes place, choose a place with few distractions, other people, or loud noises. Turn off the TV or radio and close the door. If your spouse is likely to be defensive or suspicious, choose a place in which he or she feels secure.

Also, try to talk alone and face-to-face. This will impress your partner that this is a matter of considerable importance to you. It will also allow you to interpret facial expressions and body language during the course of the conversation and permit you to clarify misunderstandings and get feedback to what you are saying before moving to other issues.

Use Wise Words

Perhaps the most important consideration in any confrontation is the actual words you use. Therefore, it is wise to sit down beforehand and plan what you will say, even jotting down key thoughts and words.

Your plan should contain these items: the issues you believe need to be addressed; the issues you want to avoid, either because they are peripheral to your main concerns or because they are likely to offend your spouse; the exact words that describe your feelings (concerned, frustrated, confused, disappointed, etc.); how the problem is affecting you; how you would prefer the problem be solved; and the ways you will both benefit from a cooperative effort to finding a solution. You should plan to use gracious, clear, and constructive words and to avoid words that will unnecessarily offend your spouse or make him or her defensive.

While you cannot write a script for your entire conversation, you can formulate your opening remarks. Make sure these set the tone for a positive encounter. You might begin by apologizing for hasty or insensitive comments that contributed to the tension between you—an initial confession often sets a positive, calm tone—or you could express concern about an issue that has arisen between the two of you. A humble and gracious opening statement tells your partner you don't want to create an argument but are seeking positive dialogue.

Also, try to anticipate how your partner will react to your comments, and plan gracious responses. Even if your partner responds differently than you thought, the very act of considering his or her reactions beforehand will generally make it easier to respond in a constructive way. Anticipate possible angry reactions and commit yourself to turning them back with gentleness. Communicate in your words and actions that you take the anger seriously and want to dig to the root problem that instigated it.

Couching your comments in "I" statements is one of the most helpful skills in defusing angry reactions. Instead of using fighting words like "You are so insensitive" or "You are so inconsiderate," turn the statement around, giving information about yourself rather than attacking your spouse. A typical formula is: "I feel _____ when you _____, because _____. As a result, _____." Here are some examples:

- "I feel hurt when you make fun of me in front of other people, because it makes me feel stupid and foolish. As a result, I am becoming reluctant to invite people over for dinner."
- "I feel frustrated that you spend so much time at the office, because then the primary responsibility for raising our children falls on me. As a result, our kids are not being raised the way God intended."
- "I am confused by your saying that I never listen, because twice last week we sat for over an hour while you shared your deep concerns with me. I don't know what to do differently."

What do "I" statements do? They tell your spouse how his or her behavior is affecting you. Putting yourself into the picture reduces his or her defensiveness and makes it more difficult to play the blame game. They also identify specifically what your spouse has done that you're concerned about; they narrow the focus and tell him or her that you're not going to insert unrelated issues into the discussion. Finally, "I" statements explain why you feel the issue is important and why you want to discuss it. Chances are, if your partner understands how you feel and what effect his or her behavior is having on you, he or she will be more willing to talk about and deal with the problem.

One final point about words: Steer well clear of exaggeration. Instead of saying to your spouse, "You're always home late from work," say instead, "You've been home late three times this week." Instead of "*Nobody* in this family wants to go *anywhere* with you anymore," say "I've gotten to the point where I'd rather not go to dinner with you." The phrases "you always," "you never," and "every time" tell your spouse that you're not being honest with him or her, and they discourage him or her from taking the rest of what you say seriously.

MINISTER WITH THE GOSPEL

Because of our sinful nature, many of us find it all too easy to point out others' errors and judge them for their mistakes. If we give in to this inclination when we confront others, it will almost always result in a stressful and unproductive conversation.

We must remember when we confront our spouse or children that we are in the same boat with them. Not only do we offend them on other, different occasions, but we all offend God with our sinful thoughts and actions. It's the way we are by nature; it's the mark we bear.

God, of course, saved us from the everlasting punishment we so justly deserve. And He wants His redeeming grace to flow through us as we relate to other people. Thus, when we must confront someone, we should resist the tendency to lecture that person with a list of God's commands and his or her failures. Instead, we should always seek to minister the gospel to the person, holding out the promise that Jesus died to deliver us from our sins, and that He delights to bless us with forgiveness and reconciliation, both with Him and with anyone we may have offended.

My wife taught me this principle when I was confronting my daughter in a thoughtless way. I had been asked to teach peacemaking to the faculty of a Christian school. Since the conference was scheduled to be held at a beautiful mountain camp, I asked Corlette and my children to join me. On the last day of the conference, my eight-year-old daughter, Megan, got into a quarrel with the daughter of the school's administrator. Since I was president of an organization called Peacemaker Ministries and since I had been using illustrations all weekend long on how my children practiced peacemaking, I felt awkward and embarrassed that my daughter was not handling the situation properly.

I immediately stepped in and started to pressure Megan to confess what she had done wrong. "Come on, Megan," I said. "You know what you should do…. Admit where you were wrong, honey…. Get the log out of your eye…. Use the Five A's (a shorter version of the Seven A's of Confession)." And finally: "Do it now!"

Unfortunately, Megan was at a stage in life where she resisted such overt pressure. The more I pushed, the more she dug in her heels. Several people were watching, and I was becoming increasingly frustrated and angry. In my pride and desire to impress people with my family's "expertise" in peacemaking, I was about to make a fool of myself.

But God had mercy on me, and He brought it through my wife. Corlette stepped to my side and whispered, "May I try to talk with her?"

"Sure, go ahead," I blurted, moving back a step.

Corlette knelt so she could look Megan in the eye. Then she gave my daughter a warm smile. She held out her hands as though offering our daughter a gift, saying, "Megan, God is offering you a way out of this. You know that you've gotten yourself into a pickle, and that things will only get worse if you play the blame game. I understand, because I've done the same thing sometimes. But we don't need to be stuck here, honey."

Holding her cupped hands a little higher in front of Megan, she continued: "Jesus is offering to help you, Megan. He died for your sins so you can be free from them. All you need to do is ask Jesus for His help, and He will forgive you and help you work this out."

Megan wavered for a moment, caught between her stubborn pride and the good news that Corlette offered. Then she burst into tears and threw herself into her mother's arms. "Oh, Mommy," she cried, "I've made such a mess. I was mean to Anna, and I've made Daddy look bad. Please help me."

Of course, it was Daddy's own pride that made him look bad. But God graciously delivered both father and daughter from their sin through Corlette's thoughtful confrontation. She gently reminded us both that the gospel is God's promise to deliver us not only from the eternal consequences of our sin, but also from the day-to-day conflicts that we get ourselves into. Once we both remembered and embraced that wonderful news, the conflict between the two little girls was quickly resolved.

The key to effective confrontation, especially with a person who professes to follow Christ, is not to hammer him or her into submission with the law. Rather, it is to give him or her hope through the gospel, which God can use to help us see where we have swerved from His path and encourage us to look to Him to get us back on track.

GETTING HELP

Even if you follow every communication principle described above, your spouse may refuse to listen to you or change the habits that are harming your marriage. If so, you have several possible courses of action. First, you can simply back off and pray for God to give you patience and continue His sanctifying work in you, regardless of what your spouse does. Second, you could seek counsel and encouragement from your pastor or another godly advisor who might be able to help you see ways that you can apply these principles more effectively (Proverbs 13:10).

Third, if the problem is serious and you see no hope of making progress through your own efforts, you could appeal to your spouse to join you in seeking counseling or mediation with someone who could help you understand each other and find a proper solution to your differences (see Matthew 18:16; we will discuss this more in chapter 11).

Finally, if your spouse refuses to participate in or respond to counseling and continues to undermine your marriage, you may appeal to the leaders of your church to intervene pursuant to Matthew 18:17 and to use redemptive church discipline to promote repentance and preserve your marriage. As the story on pages 180-182 [see chapter 11] shows, this is not an easy or pleasant process, but when all else fails, it is a legitimate step to take to save a threatened marriage.

AS YOU GROW

If you are presently involved in a conflict, these questions will help you to apply the principles presented in this chapter.

1. Do you believe that your spouse has sinned against you in this situation? If so, is it too serious to overlook? More specifically:
    a. Is it dishonoring God? How?
    b. Is it damaging your relationship with your spouse? How?
    c. Is it hurting others? How?
    d. Is it hurting your spouse? How?
    e. Is it making him or her less useful to the Lord?

2. Are there any sins you need to confess before confronting your spouse?

3. What can you do and say that would clearly communicate your love and concern for your spouse?

4. Which listening skills do you have a hard time with: waiting, attending, clarifying, reflecting, or agreeing? Write down some things you will do or say to overcome these weaknesses.

5. What is the best time and place to talk with your spouse?

6. How can you demonstrate to your spouse that you believe the best about him or her?

7. Write a brief summary of what you need to say or avoid saying. Include:
    a. The issues that you believe should be addressed.
    b. Words and topics to avoid.
    c. Words that describe your feelings.
    d. A description of the effect the dispute is having on you and others ("I" statements).
    e. Your suggestions and preferences for a solution.

      f.   The benefits that will be produced by cooperating to find a solution.

      g.   Your opening statement.

8. How can you specifically minister the gospel to your spouse as you talk about this situation?

9. Go on record with the Lord by writing a prayer based on the principles taught in this chapter.

DIGGING DEEPER

▌ Chapters 7–9 of *The Peacemaker: A Biblical Guide to Resolving Personal Conflict* provide more detailed information on effective confrontation. These chapters explain how to decide whether an offense is too serious to overlook, how to confront non-Christians or people in authority, and how to enlist other Christians and even church discipline to promote needed changes in a marriage.

▌ Paul Tripp's book *The War of Words* provides key insights on confrontation by explaining the relationship between the idols of our hearts and the words that flow from our mouths.

▌ People will receive our confrontation much more readily if we first listen to what they have to say about us. For helpful guidance on how to model a humble response to confrontation, see the article by Alfred Poirier in Appendix F, "The Cross and Criticism."

6

Forgiveness

John took the hand of his wife, Sarah, and looked into her eyes. His face was somber, his eyes remorseful. "What I said at the dinner table last night was totally uncalled for," he said. "I am sorry that I said those things about you to the Cooks and the Cantwells. I felt awful afterward, and I knew immediately that I shouldn't have said it."

Sarah brushed him off. "It's okay," she said. "You are who you are, John. I'm used to it."

"No, no, Sarah. Let me finish." He gave her hand a tender squeeze. "I made some comments about you that were very unkind. Comments about your driving, comments about your cooking. I guess I wanted attention. You know, being the funny man and all that. But those cracks were cold, they were untrue, and I shouldn't have said them. I saw immediately that they embarrassed you. I am terribly sorry." He paused. "Will you forgive me, please?"

"Look, it's not a problem. I didn't even notice."

"It's important to me that you know I realize I was wrong."

"Yeah, sure. I forgive you. Like I said, no problem."

"OK. That means a lot to me," John said. "Thanks."

A couple days later, on a Saturday, Sarah blew into the kitchen while John was drinking his coffee and reading the paper. "Ah," said John, looking up. "If it isn't the woman I love and cherish." He rose to embrace her.

She had time only for a drive-by hug, on her hurried way out the door. "Sorry, honey. Jenny's already late for the science fair at school. Gotta go."

"You're going to drive her?"

Sarah stopped. "If that's okay," she said.

John smiled warmly. "Yeah, sure." He paused. "Of course it's okay, honey."

"You won't be worried if I change lanes on my own?"

"Huh?"

Sarah had an unfailing ear—she quoted her husband directly from a couple of nights before. "When Sarah hits her turn signal to switch lanes," she said in a mimicking voice, "everybody in the car checks the blind spot."

"I said I was sorry about that," John said.

Sarah laughed. "Lighten up, will you? It's a joke, all right?"

John forced a laugh.

"Well, gotta go," Sarah said. And she was out the door.

Tuesday night they had Sarah's parents over for dinner. On the menu were pork chops.

"These chops are absolutely delicious, Sarah," John said after his first mouthful. The rest of the table chimed in—"Yeah, great, Mom!" "Sure thick and juicy, Sarah!"

Sarah speared the chop from her own plate with her fork. She lifted it to her eyes and pretended to examine it closely. "Won't be able to play Frisbee with these things, huh, John?"

Everybody laughed. Except John. Probably because he had heard the joke before—indeed, he had told it about the chops Sarah had prepared the previous week for the Cooks and the Cantwells.

That night as they were getting ready for bed, John said, "Dinner was great, honey."

She was leaning over the bathroom sink, washing her face. "Glad you liked it."

"You said some funny things, too."

"Well, I've learned from the best."

"That joke about the pork chop was kind of a low blow, though," John said.

"You mean I said something to hurt your feelings, John?" She looked at him whimsically in the mirror.

"Actually, what I meant was, I was hoping you had forgiven me for that."

She turned off the faucet and began her trek to her side of the bed. "It was a joke, John. You have got to chill out a little."

"Well, okay, but…"

She got into bed and pulled up the covers and turned to face the wall.

John sat on his side of the bed. "Sarah," he said, "it seems like things haven't been the same between us lately."

No response.

"Ever since I made those cracks last week at dinner, things have been kind of chilly between us, it seems."

Sarah turned her head. "John, I've forgotten about that."

"I mean, I don't know, Sarah. Things just seem different."

"You're imagining things."

John got in bed and threw his arm around his wife. "Can we talk about it a little bit, honey? I want to make sure everything's okay between us."

She turned her head back toward the wall. "Nothing to talk about, John. Everything's okay. I forgive you… Now, I'm pretty tired, so…"

"You're sure about that, now?"

She grunted.

"You *do* forgive me and everything."

Another grunt.

"Okay." John sighed and stared at the back of his wife's head for a moment. Then he kissed her hair and turned off the bedside light.

■ ■ ■

Sarah presents us with the antithesis of proper forgiveness. She may have said the right words, but her actions revealed her heart. John's jokes obviously cut her more deeply than she let on. Her continual expression of forgiveness notwithstanding, the fact that she kept flinging his comments back in his face proved that her forgiveness was neither complete nor sincere. She couldn't let the incident go. And in that, she is like many of us.

Because Christians are the most forgiven people in the world, we should be the most forgiving people in the world as well. That's the theory anyway. God forgives us perfectly and completely, and He calls us to forgive our brothers and sisters in like manner. But in practice it doesn't turn out that way. The forgiveness we offer others is often far from complete, and it frequently fails to match the marvelous forgiveness that God bestows on us.

Since we are not God, we cannot forgive exactly as God forgives. The forgiveness we offer to others falls short of God's perfect and pure forgiveness of us. There will be always be a taint of lack of forgiveness to it, a sinful inclination to dwell on the sin and hold it against our fellow Christian.

That, simply, is the legacy Adam and Eve left us with in the Garden of Eden. But when we remember our position before God, when we adopt an attitude of continual repentance and thankfulness for our salvation, God will help us, through the work of His Spirit, to improve our ability to forgive others. When we come daily before our Lord and repent of our sins, seeking God's forgiveness and the Holy Spirit's strength to improve our lives, our forgiveness of others will grow as well; it will become more sincere and more lasting the more we seek God's grace and guidance.

This is our hope. Let us look more closely at how we can put forgiveness into practice when we have the opportunity to forgive someone.

THE FOUR PROMISES OF FORGIVENESS

Before we can talk about what forgiveness is, and how we can more completely forgive our spouse or children, let's talk about what it is not. First, forgiveness is not a feeling; it's not like love, hate, jealousy, envy, or lust. In fact, we should set forgiveness apart from our feelings altogether. To be sure, deciding to forgive can eventually change our feelings tremendously, but that comes later, after we've made the conscious decision to forgive.

Second, forgiveness is not forgetting. God doesn't forget our sins when He forgives them. He decides not to remember them; not to mention, recount, or think about them ever again; not to hold them against us in the final ledger. Similarly, when we forgive, we must consciously try not to think or talk about what others have done that hurt us. This is, of course, no easy task, especially when the hurt is fresh in our minds. But through God's help, accompanied by a continual awareness of His immeasurable forgiveness for us, painful memories of others' wrongs usually fade with time.

And third, forgiveness is not excusing. We do not simply sweep our spouse's behavior under the rug when we forgive, in effect saying, "You really didn't do anything wrong" or "You couldn't help it." On the contrary, the fact that we forgive indicates that a sin was committed. (Excusing and overlooking are appropriate, however, if someone has merely made a mistake—when there is no moral implication to the action, such as accidentally breaking a dish or inadvertently providing a wrong telephone number.)

That's what forgiveness is not. Now, what is it? Forgiveness is an act of the will, a decision not to think or talk about what someone has done. It is an active process involving a conscious choice and a deliberate course of action. It is the canceling of a debt that your spouse has incurred because of improper behavior or words. And just as God's forgiveness of us breaks down the wall we erected between Him and us by our sin, our forgiveness of our spouse opens the way for a renewed relationship with him or her. It brings us back together after an offense has separated us from each other.

As we discussed in chapter 3, one way to put these concepts into action is to think of forgiveness as a set of four promises. When we forgive someone, we make these four pledges:

- I will not think about this incident.
- I will not bring up this incident again and use it against you.
- I will not talk to others about this incident.
- I will not allow this incident to stand between us or hinder our personal relationship.

In my wife's book for children, *The Young Peacemaker,* Corlette has summarized these promises in a short, memorable rhyme: "Good thought, hurt you not, gossip never, friends forever." Regardless of the form you use, God calls us to commit ourselves to forgive others as He has forgiven us.

Sarah, in our opening illustration, managed to break all four promises. She continued to dwell on her husband's comments at the dinner party. She brought his offense up repeatedly and threw it back in his face, both privately and in front of others. And her coldness when they went to bed showed that the incident had become a barrier between them.

It sounds familiar, doesn't it? We all know how difficult it is to forgive others. In some cases it is impossible to even think about making the four promises stated above, much less to keep them. Fortunately, God promises to help us in this task. Through the Bible He offers guidance, and through His Spirit strength, for us to put into effect the forgiveness He desires of us. And by appropriating His guidance and grace, we can surmount some of the common roadblocks that arise in our path toward forgiveness.

OVERCOMING UNFORGIVENESS
Confirm Repentance

Sometimes the problems that prevent forgiveness do not lie with the forgiver but with the offender. Many Christians take a casual attitude toward repentance, either not understanding what true repentance entails or attempting to dismiss their wrongs with shallow and superficial words.

During a conference Corlette and I attended, I thoughtlessly criticized her in front of a group of people. When we were alone later in the day, Corlette let me know it bothered her. I casually replied, "I'm sorry. That was wrong of me. Will you forgive me?" She said sure, she forgave me, but a few hours later it was obvious that the matter was still on her mind. She wanted to talk about it; she was having a hard time forgiving me.

When I agreed to talk it through, she told me she didn't think I understood how deeply I had hurt her with my remarks. Then she explained how I had embarrassed her. And she was right. I didn't understand the full effect of my words on her. My confession had been quite deficient (I had missed four of the Seven A's of Confession). After hearing her out, I confessed more thoroughly and committed myself, with God's help, to be more sensitive in the future. After that, Corlette found it much easier to forgive me.

Confession is such an emphasized part of our theology, and of the peacemaking process, that its very commonness may lead us to minimize its importance. Confession is the answer to so many interpersonal problems that we can take it for granted, just as we often take God's forgiveness of us for granted. We must take repentance seriously when we confess our sins to God, never brushing them aside as something unimportant. And repentance among married couples should be taken equally seriously. If you are having trouble forgiving your spouse, you may need to go to him or her, the way Corlette did to me. When repentance is sincere and complete, you should find it much easier to forgive and be reconciled.

But what do you do if your spouse refuses to repent of a sin? If it was only a minor offense, you may to choose to forgive unconditionally, making all four promises of forgiveness. But if the offense is too serious to overlook, you may have to approach forgiveness in stages.

The first stage is to commit yourself to maintaining a loving and merciful attitude toward your spouse no matter what he or she does (see Luke 6:27-29). In doing so, you are imitating God's merciful attitude toward us even before we repent of our sins (Luke 23:34). You may think of this as making the first promise of forgiveness, which means you will not dwell on the hurt or desire vengeance. Instead, by God's grace, you will keep yourself in a "position of forgiveness," praying for your spouse, showing gentleness and kindness, and being ready to pursue complete reconciliation as soon as he or she repents. This attitude keeps the door wide open for complete forgiveness, and also guards you from being eaten up by bitterness and resentment.

Until your spouse repents, you should ask God for wisdom on how to help him or her see the wrong. At the very least, you should be praying regularly for your spouse, asking God to open his or her heart and eyes. It may include deliberate acts of kindness that God may use to soften your partner's heart (Romans 12:19-21). But it may also involve carefully planned and loving confrontation at opportune moments, as we discussed in chapter 5 (see Luke 17:3; 2 Timothy 2:24-26).

If the offense is serious and delayed repentance will do further harm, you may need to ask a godly couple or a leader in your church to meet with you and your spouse to help you put the matter completely to rest (see Matthew 18:16). When repentance finally occurs, you can joyfully make all four promises of forgiveness and experience together the forgiveness made possible through Christ.

Renounce Sinful Attitudes and Expectations

Another roadblock to forgiveness is our own sinful attitudes and expectations. Although we are completely forgiven by God without doing anything to deserve it, we often fail to give the same grace to those who need our forgiveness. We haven't earned our forgiveness, but we sure want our spouse to earn his or hers. Related obstacles to forgiveness may include a desire to make our spouse suffer for his or her offenses, or an unspoken expectation that he or she must somehow guarantee to *never* commit that offense again.

Remember God's Forgiveness

God places no such conditions on His forgiveness. He doesn't require that we earn it, nor does He demand guarantees of future sinlessness (we'd be in pretty bad shape if He did). Instead, whenever we confess our sins, "He is faithful and just and will forgive us our sins and purify us from all unrighteousness" (1 John 1:9).

The key to overcoming obstacles to forgiveness is God's own example. His free gift of salvation is the foundation for how we relate to others, especially when they have wronged us. When we remember His unsurpassed love and mercy toward us, this should inspire us to treat others the same way. "Be kind and compassionate to one another, forgiving each other, just as in Christ God forgave you" (Ephesians 4:32). Therefore, in response to God's love, we need to renounce our sinful attitudes and expectations and ask Him to help us forgive others.

Jesus' parable of the unmerciful servant in Matthew 18 vividly illustrates this principle. A servant owed his king an enormous sum, and when the king threatened to sell the man and his family into slavery to pay the debt, the servant threw himself on the king's mercy. This moved the king, and he "took pity on him, canceled the debt and let him go" (v. 27).

Soon thereafter the servant came across a man who owed him some money—not nearly so much as the servant had owed the king. When that man begged for time to repay the debt, the servant refused and had him thrown into prison until he could repay it (v. 30).

The king heard about it and called the servant to his court. Then he said, "You wicked servant.... I canceled all that debt of yours because you begged me to. Shouldn't you have had mercy on your fellow servant just as I had on you?" (vv. 32-33). Then the king "turned him over to the jailers to be tortured, until he should pay back all he owed" (v. 34).

This parable puts our refusal to forgive others into a little different perspective, doesn't it? After all, our debt to God far surpasses anything as trivial as money; it involves our very lives, both on this earth and in eternity. Therefore, if we are experiencing trouble forgiving someone, we should remember God's love for us and ask Him for grace to imitate the forgiveness He has given us through His Son.

Practice the Replacement Principle

Another practical way to overcome obstacles to forgiveness is to practice the "replacement principle." As we mentioned above, our forgiveness of others should be modeled after God's forgiveness of us. He doesn't bring up our sins after we confess them; rather, He decides not to remember them. This is not an easy thing to imitate. If someone has deeply hurt us, memories of that offense may keep popping back into our minds days or weeks afterward.

This is where the replacement principle comes in. If we can't stop thinking about an offense committed against us, we should consciously *replace* that negative thought with a positive one. Every time we begin to brood over the incident, we should ask for God's help and deliberately pray for that person or think of something positive about the offender. As the apostle Paul wrote in Philippians 4:8, "Finally, brothers, whatever is true, whatever is noble, whatever is right, whatever is pure, whatever is lovely, whatever is admirable—if anything is excellent or praiseworthy—think about such things."

The replacement principle applies not only to our thoughts, but also to our speech and actions. If you want to accelerate forgiveness, make it a point to speak graciously about your spouse when his or her name comes up in discussions with others. Express appreciation for things he or she has done and focus on his or her good qualities.

As for actions, C. S. Lewis summed it up well when he wrote in his classic *Mere Christianity*, "When you are behaving as if you loved someone, you will presently come to love him."[1] It may sound far-fetched, even irrational, but it's true. I have experienced this process over and over again.

Once I quarreled with Corlette over a trivial matter and had not truly forgiven her. Then she asked me to make a grocery run, which I don't like to do. I grudgingly pushed my cart around the store, brooding all the while. When I went down the coffee aisle, I saw some special coffee Corlette loves to drink. I thought, *If she hadn't been so unkind to me, I'd surprise her with a bag of this coffee.*

Even while I was thinking those words, another part of me wanted to buy the coffee for her. I picked up the bag, just to check the price, and the moment I touched it I started to have a change of heart. My resentment melted away and I felt a flush of love for my wife and the desire to see her happy face when I presented the gift to her. I bought it, and we were fully reconciled shortly after I got home. The surprising thing was that in the process of giving her a gift, my heart was changed.

A FORGIVENESS STORY

The story about Sarah and John at the beginning of this chapter showed us how *not* to forgive. I would like to end the chapter with another story, one that demonstrates how God's redeeming love and grace enabled a man to forgive one of the worst sins that can take place in a marriage.

When Rick came to see me, discovery of his wife's adultery was already a month behind him. Even though Pam had given every evidence of repentance and had begged him to forgive her, Rick could not do it.

Rick was a Christian, so he knew he should forgive Pam. He appeased his conscience by saying, "I forgive you, but I can't ever be close to you again." This only heightened the hopelessness of the situation, and soon they both thought that divorce was the only way to end their misery.

I saw that Rick's bitterness was one of the primary contributing factors to the destruction of their marriage. His empty "forgiveness" had no power to dispel the memory of Pam's unfaithfulness, which hung like a dark cloud over the relationship. He could put the past behind them only by true forgiveness, only through the rich, redeeming, thoroughly cleansing forgiveness described in Scripture and modeled by Jesus.

I said, "Rick, imagine that you had just confessed a serious sin to God, and that He responded audibly, saying, 'I forgive you, Rick, but I can't ever be close to you again.' How would that make you feel?"

After an awkward pause, he replied, "I guess I'd feel like God hadn't really forgiven me."

"But isn't that exactly the way you are forgiving Pam?" I asked. Rick looked at the floor, wrestling for an answer.

I continued gently, "Imagine if instead God said, 'Rick, *I promise* never to think about your sin again, or to dwell on it or brood over it. *I promise* never to bring it up and use it against you. *I promise* not to talk to others about it. And *I promise* not to let it stand between us or hinder our personal relationship.'"

After a long silence, tears began to fill Rick's eyes. "I would know I was completely forgiven.... But I wouldn't deserve that kind of forgiveness after the way I've treated Pam."

"Would you ever deserve it?" I asked. "God's forgiveness is a free gift, purchased for you by Jesus' death on the cross. He doesn't forgive you because you've earned it. He forgives you to display His glory and the riches of His grace. When you truly understand how precious and undeserved His forgiveness is, you will want to forgive Pam the same way He has forgiven you."

"I know I *should*," he answered, "but how could I ever keep the four promises you just described? I can't imagine forgetting what Pam did! And I just don't feel like I could ever be close to her again."

"Where does the Bible say that forgiveness is forgetting ... or that it depends on feelings?" I asked. "Forgiveness is an act of the will, Rick, a decision you make in spite of your feelings. Of course it's hard, especially in a case like this. But if you ask for God's help as you make those four promises to Pam, He will give you the grace to follow through on them."

We talked for a half hour longer and then we prayed, and Rick's doubts and fear subsided. An hour later he met with Pam to confess his sin of bitterness and unforgiveness.

When she repeated how sorry she was, he said this: "Honey, I want to forgive you the way God has forgiven me. With His help, I promise not to dwell on this anymore. I promise never to bring it up and use it against you. I promise not to talk to others about it. And I promise not to let it stand between us or hinder our relationship."

Pam fell sobbing into his arms. Rick's commitment to forgiveness marked the beginning of their healing process. They would still spend many hours in counseling to address the root causes of their marital problems, but a couple weeks later Rick told me that the four promises were already working.

"After I promised not to think about Pam's sin," he said, "I realized that the burden had shifted to me. Now when I catch myself thinking about what she did, I confess to God that I am breaking my word. I ask for His help and then focus my thoughts on the immensity of His forgiveness toward me or on Pam's good qualities.

"I praise God for His healing. The negative memories have started to fade, and I am beginning to love my wife again!"

Sins, even terribly hurtful ones, can happen in families, where our relationships are especially close and a sense of betrayal can be particularly intense. But thanks be to God, forgiveness happens as well. His love is so strong that He erases our sins from His ledger, having nailed them to the cross. And He gives us grace to imitate His love by promising to forgive others the same way He has forgiven us. When we draw on that grace and live out these promises, we can restore precious relationships and at the same time bring glory and honor to the One who makes our forgiveness possible.

AS YOU GROW

If you are presently involved in a conflict, these questions will help you to apply the principles presented in this chapter.

1. How has your spouse sinned against you?

2. Which of these sins has he or she confessed?

3. Write out the four promises that you will make to your spouse at this time to indicate your forgiveness.

4. Which of the unconfessed sins can you overlook and forgive at this time? (Those that cannot be overlooked will have to be dealt with by applying the principles taught in chapter 5.)

5. If you are having a hard time forgiving your spouse:
    a. Is it because you are not sure he or she has repented? If so, how could you encourage confirmation of repentance?
    b. Do you think he or she must somehow earn or deserve your forgiveness? Are you trying to punish by withholding forgiveness? Are you expecting a guarantee that the offense will not happen again? If you have any of these attitudes or expectations, what do you need to do?
    c. How did your sins contribute to the conflict? How can you imitate God's forgiveness?
    d. Read Matthew 18:21-35. What is the point of this passage? How does it apply to you?

6. How can you demonstrate forgiveness or promote reconciliation:
    a. In thought?
    b. In word?
    c. In deed?

7. Go on record with the Lord by writing a prayer based on the principles taught in this chapter.

DIGGING DEEPER

Chapter 10 of *The Peacemaker: A Biblical Guide to Resolving Personal Conflict* provides more detailed information on forgiveness, explaining what to do if someone refuses to repent, when and how to apply consequences that will encourage change, and how to overcome unforgiveness and promote genuine reconciliation even when terrible sins have occurred. Chapter 12 explains how to relate to people who continue to do evil even when you have made every effort to be reconciled.

7

Negotiation

In the previous chapters we have focused on resolving *personal issues* between spouses. These issues involve the relational aspects of our marriage, how we treat and feel about each other. Relationships that have been damaged by sinful words or actions require the steps detailed in the three previous chapters: confession, confrontation, and forgiveness.

Marital conflicts can also arise over *substantive issues*. For example: Where will we spend our vacation? Where will we send the kids to school? How often will we eat out? How will we discipline the kids? Should we buy a dog? Who picks the new car?

As we have all experienced, substantive conflicts can easily turn into volatile personal conflicts. The original issue (such as "Where will we spend our vacation?") may be completely obscured by careless words, critical judgments, hurt feelings, and a lingering sense of bitterness and resentment. Whenever this happens, we will be faced with a conflict that is both substantive and personal.

In this chapter we will study a negotiation model that can reduce personal tensions and offenses, and at the same time enable us to find mutually satisfactory agreement on difficult substantive issues. But before we look at the model itself, we should discuss the *spirit* in which we should pursue negotiation.

COOPERATIVE VERSUS COMPETITIVE NEGOTIATION

The will to win, it can be argued, is one of the things that makes America great. Competition is the bedrock of our economic system and the basis of nearly all sports.

A competitive attitude is seldom beneficial in a marriage, however. God intends for a husband and wife to be of "one flesh." Therefore, we should be complementing and fulfilling each other, not trying to out-maneuver each other to get our own way.

When couples give in to a competitive attitude, they are unlikely to find the best solution to a problem. By working against each other, focusing on surface issues and neglecting underlying needs and desires, they will often reach superficial solutions.

Competitive negotiating can also take a significant toll on personal relationships. When we insist on getting our own way on a substantive issue, we can send the message that we do not care about our spouse's needs or feelings. And if we push hard to win on substantive issues, we can damage feelings even further through insensitive or manipulative words or by judging our spouse's motives or values.

These pitfalls are more easily avoided when we use a *cooperative* approach to negotiation. Instead of each side trying to get his or her way, they can seek solutions that are beneficial to everyone involved. As both spouses' underlying needs and concerns are considered, they are more likely to strengthen their relationship while at the same time developing wise and mutually beneficial solutions.

Not surprisingly, the Bible repeatedly commends a cooperative approach to negotiating. In Philippians 2:3-4, the apostle Paul teaches that we should "Do nothing out of selfish ambition or vain conceit, but in humility consider others better than yourselves. Each of you should look not only to your own interests, but also to the interests of others." This attitude of being concerned about others' needs as well as your own is commanded in many other passages, including Matthew 7:12 ("Do to others what you would have them do to you"), Matthew 22:39 ("Love your neighbor as yourself"), and 1 Corinthians 13:5 ("Love…is not self-seeking"). If these passages apply in general to all of our relationships, how much more should they apply within our marriage!

These passages do not require that you automatically give in to every desire of your spouse. Note that Philippians 2:4 teaches that we may legitimately look out for our own interests even as we consider the interests of others. But when we do look out for our own interests, we should not do so with "selfish ambition or vain conceit," but with a humble spirit that shows respect and concern for our partner's perspective. To put it another way, God wants us to approach negotiation with love and wisdom. With love for your spouse, you gather relevant information about the dispute and explore creative options, seeking wisdom to find a solution that honors God and benefits both you and your spouse. Such a resolution comes through cooperation, not competition.

Having negotiated hundreds of family, church, business, and legal conflicts, I have found that successful cooperative negotiation is usually comprised of five steps, which I summarize as the PAUSE principle. This acronym stands for:

- **P**repare
- **A**ffirm relationships
- **U**nderstand interests
- **S**earch for creative solutions
- **E**valuate options objectively and reasonably

If you carefully follow each of these steps, you will usually reach mutually beneficial agreements on the substantive issues that arise in your marriage. Let's see how a wife could follow this process as she seeks to resolve a significant substantive conflict with her husband.

WHEN YOU NEED TO NEGOTIATE, PAUSE

Gary and Alice, like all Christian couples, desire to nurture the spiritual side of life. Over the past couple years, however, tension has developed in their marriage over the matter of spiritual leadership. Alice has been deeply concerned about her husband's inconsistency in leading the family spiritually. They have talked about the issue repeatedly, but still the problem lingers.

Typically, Alice brings up the issue following some difficulty in family life. One of their children uses bad language; the other gets in trouble at school for fighting; both want to watch TV programs that aren't very wholesome; both try to fake illnesses to get out of going to church and Sunday school. Troubled by these problems, Alice broaches the topic of spiritual leadership to Gary, usually in a critical way. "You know, Gary, this wouldn't happen so much if we sat down and studied the Bible together, like a family is supposed to…. Our kids would be a lot better off if their father assumed his rightful place as the spiritual head of this family."

In reaction, Gary grows defensive. He can't argue that he *shouldn't* lead the family spiritually—he knows the Bible well enough to realize that's not even debatable. His problem is time. Or his job. Or how tired he is at the end of the day. Or how early he has to be in to work in the morning. Or his out-of-town trips. He always has some excuse.

Even so, whenever Alice confronts him, Gary usually tries to be more consistent in leading family devotions and praying with the kids in the morning. But it lasts only a few days. Soon things begin to slide back to where they had been before.

This eventually precipitates another confrontation from Alice, more excuses from Gary, and family devotions for a couple days before life in their household returns to the same old routine.

Let's see what happened in this situation when Alice gave up her haphazard approach to the problem and thoughtfully applied the PAUSE principle.

Prepare

Alice prepared to approach Gary by considering how to apply the Four G's (see chapter 3) to her situation. She began by asking the foundational question, "How can I glorify God in this situation?" (the first G). She realized that the best way to do this was to keep her eyes fixed on Jesus, looking for ways to treat Gary the same way God was treating her, with selfless love and forgiveness.

She asked God to help her get the log out of her own eye (the second G). As she prayed, she realized that she had allowed a good desire (Gary being a spiritual leader) to grow into a controlling demand. She also realized that she had condemned Gary in her heart for his inconsistency in this area, spoken to him out of frustration rather than love, and had been disrespectful toward him in front of their children.

Next, she prayed for wisdom on how to go to Gary to discuss the situation and seek reconciliation with him (the third and fourth G's). She prayed that God would help her to understand the pressures Gary was under and why it was difficult for him to be consistent in his leadership. She also tried to discern the real cause of their conflict. Since Gary agreed that he should be the spiritual leader of the family, the real questions seemed to be *To what degree should he be involved in spiritual teaching?* and *How can we work together to overcome the obstacles that limit his involvement?*

She then made a preliminary list of the various interests that Gary probably had in this situation, which included having a clear conscience before God, the satisfaction of serving his family, her approval, time to do his work, and peace and quiet at home. With these interests in mind, she thought of some possible solutions. She talked with other godly women to see how they had handled this issue in their families. She even found some books and tapes that laid out realistic plans for spiritual nurturing in the home.

She thought about when and where to initiate a conversation with Gary. She did not want to repeat her mistake of approaching him when she was exasperated or when he was tired and distracted. Instead, she planned for a time when she would be calm and when Gary would be relaxed and likely to be receptive to a discussion.

Alice also thought through her opening words to Gary, wanting to set a positive and respectful tone for their conversation, and tried to anticipate and plan for some of the ways that he might react. Finally, when she was as prepared as she could be, she committed the entire process to God in the spirit of 2 Timothy 2:24-26, asking Him to help her remember that her only job was to respectfully appeal to her husband, and that the final results were in the Lord's hands.

Affirm Relationships

Alice realized that during her previous conversations with Gary, she had focused so intently on the issue of spiritual leadership that she had sent the message that she did not care about Gary's concerns, limitations, and feelings. No wonder he was so defensive about the subject! To avoid repeating this mistake, she resolved to make a deliberate effort to affirm her love, concern, and respect for Gary throughout their next conversation.

She showed respect for Gary by asking, not demanding, that he set aside some time to discuss his spiritual leadership in their home. She asked him to choose the time and place.

When they finally sat down together, she said, "I love you, Gary, and one of the best days in my life was the day I married you. I appreciate how you have provided for our family, putting in long hours on the job to make sure we always have everything we need, and then some. You have been a great husband to me and a great father to our children, showing all of us your love in so many ways.

"I know we have discussed the spiritual life of our children many times, and I'm ashamed to realize that I have often approached you with a critical spirit and a judgmental heart. I apologize and ask your forgiveness. I hope we can discuss this issue again today, but this time I want to work with you to find a solution that is right before God and works for you. But whatever we decide, I want you to know that I recognize and respect your role as spiritual head of this household. And I will submit to your leadership regardless of what we decide."

Alice reinforced her love and concern for Gary throughout their conversation by maintaining a gentle demeanor, listening carefully to his words, asking sincere questions to understand his concerns more fully, and showing respect for his views, even if she disagreed on some points. She also continued to express genuine appreciation for all he was trying to do as he juggled the competing demands of work and family.

Not surprisingly, Gary responded favorably to her affirmation. He opened up and shared how guilty he felt for not being a more consistent spiritual leader, and he was less defensive when Alice offered insights on the problem and suggestions on how to solve it. As a result, for the first time, they began to make real progress on this issue.

Understand Interests

Before we discuss Alice's application of the third step in the PAUSE principle (understanding interests), we need to distinguish three words: *issues*, *positions*, and *interests*.

An *issue* is a concrete question that has to be addressed in order to reach an agreement. In the past, the issue that divided Alice and Gary was the kind of spiritual leadership Gary should provide for his family.

A *position* is a desired outcome or answer to the issue. Alice's position had usually been, "He should lead the family in prayer every morning, devotions at the dinner table, and one night of family study each week." Gary's position had been, "I will try to lead when I can, but you all have to understand that some days I'm running late for work in the morning or just too tired to do anything when I come home." As these two perspectives show, conflict usually involves contradictory positions. Each person proposes a different solution, and when their positions don't mesh, they end up in a tug of war to see which person will manipulate or overpower the other.

If a couple continues to focus on their competing positions, they will usually make little progress toward a meaningful solution. What they need to do is take their eyes off their positions and explore their *interests*. An interest may be a concern, desire, need, limitation, or something a person values or fears; it is anything that motivates a person. Successful negotiation requires that we seek to understand one another's underlying interests and work together to find mutually acceptable ways to meet as many of them as we can. This is why Paul says, "Each of you should look not only to your own interests, but also to the interests of others" (Philippians 2:4).

The Bible provides many colorful stories to show the importance of understanding others' interests. One of my favorites is the story of Abigail, which is found in 1 Samuel 25.

David had fled with a group of followers into the desert after King Saul tried to kill him. As they camped out in the hills, David's men protected local farmers from bandits and marauders. One of these farmers was a wealthy man named Nabal. Eventually David's supplies ran low, so he sent a delegation to Nabal to ask him for food in return for the protection David had provided. Nabal rudely refused the request and insulted David. When David heard of the insult, he called four hundred men to arms and set out to destroy Nabal and all the men who served him.

In the meantime, Nabal's wife, Abigail, heard what her husband had done and realized that David would probably be insulted. Fearing an attack, she set out to intercept David and his men and to seek peace. She loaded up several donkeys with food (good preparation and affirmation!) and met David as he descended from the hills. She approached him with great humility and clearly affirmed her concern and respect for David.

Instead of confronting David with her own position ("You should not murder innocent people") or focusing on her own interests ("If you kill all of our workers, we will be left defenseless and without support"), she focused her attention entirely on *David's interests* in the matter. She knew that his clean record and honorable reputation before God and the people of Israel were vital to him, especially when compared to the bloody record of King Saul. She realized that David risked losing God's blessing and love of the people if he stained his hands with innocent blood. Through a brilliant appeal, she shrewdly and tactfully reminded David of these interests (see 1 Samuel 25:22-31).

Even though David was backed by four hundred armed men, Abigail's appeal stopped him in his tracks. He lowered his sword and said, "Praise be to the LORD, the God of Israel, who has sent you today to meet me. May you be blessed for your good judgment and for keeping me from bloodshed this day and from avenging myself with my own hands.... Go home in peace. I have heard your words and granted your request" (1 Samuel 25:32-33, 35).

Abigail's appeal is a perfect illustration of Ecclesiastes 9:16: "Wisdom is better than strength." It also illustrates a key principle in cooperative negotiation: The more fully you understand your spouse's interests, the more persuasive and effective you can be in negotiating an agreement.

Looking again at our modern example, how could Alice apply this principle as she negotiates with her husband? She started by trying to understand the various interests that Gary was attempting to balance as he served his family and his employer. Drawing on all that she knew about her husband, she made a tentative list of his possible interests, which included:

- A desire to obey God's command to be a spiritual leader, to see his children mature in their faith and be prepared for life.
- A desire to be more disciplined himself and to have a clear conscience before the Lord as he fulfills his spiritual responsibilities.
- A desire for Alice's respect and approval (and a fear of her criticism and judgment).
- A desire to have sufficient time, energy, and flexibility to be successful in his job.
- A desire to have some time to rest and relax.

Alice realized that Gary had only a limited number of hours in his day and a limited amount of physical and mental energy to share with those who depended on him. She also discerned that he was limited by a lack of self-discipline, and by the fact that he found more pleasure in watching television at night than he did in leading family devotions. All of these factors would need to be taken into account as she tried to help him find a workable way to lead their family.

When Alice sat down to talk with Gary, she did not assume that she knew all of his interests. Instead, she asked questions and listened carefully to discern his concerns and perspectives on how he could fulfill his responsibilities. As Alice demonstrated a genuine interest in what he was thinking and feeling, Gary was even more motivated to share his heart with her, and also to try to understand his wife's concerns. They soon discovered that they had similar concerns and goals for their family's spiritual development. Both of them wanted their children to be growing in their faith, and they agreed that Gary's leadership was vital to that process. The question was, how could they work together to enable him to overcome the habits and limitations that had kept him from fulfilling his role as spiritual leader of the family?

Search for Creative Solutions

When you start to identify similar or compatible interests, it is time to move to the fourth step of the PAUSE principle: searching for creative solutions. This is the time for creative, prayerful thinking, otherwise known as brainstorming. To encourage imagination and creativity, both spouses should agree to consider *any* idea that comes to mind. No suggestion is wrong at this stage, nor is there only one answer to the problem. Steer clear of evaluating the effectiveness of any of the ideas—that comes later. During this phase you simply want to get as many ideas on the table as possible without critiquing them.

Brainstorming can also involve discussing the obstacles that have contributed to the problem in the past. Do any of our daily habits get in the way of solving this problem? Is the way responsibilities are divided up between us a contributing factor? Getting these factors on the table clarifies the discussion and makes it more practical.

When Alice and Gary reached this stage in their negotiation, Alice asked whether they could discuss some of the obstacles that had impeded the family's spiritual growth in the past. Both came up with a number of points. As in most households, school mornings were crazy. Alice had enough trouble making sure her kids were wearing matching socks when they went out the door, much less sitting them down for quiet prayer. To complicate matters, both Alice and Gary often stayed up late watching television and consequently would get up late the next morning. So even when they had planned a morning devotional period, it got lost in the shuffle.

Then there was Gary's schedule. He had to work late frequently and didn't return home on those evenings until 7:00 or 7:30 P.M., well after the family ate dinner. Thus they couldn't take advantage of the natural setting of the dinner table for devotions. Moreover, he was invariably tired and not in the mood to lead the family at those times. On the days he left work on time, he had so many chores to do around the house—fixing things, doing the family finances, etc.—that it wasn't until late in the evening, after the kids were in bed, that he even had a chance to think about family devotions. Plus, his job required him to leave town frequently for three or four days at a time.

Then there were the kids. Once they finished their dinner, they squirmed in their chairs, played with the tableware, and pleaded to be excused so they could play. So expert were they at this that Gary and Alice often relented to the pressure simply so they could eat in peace. After-dinner devotions in that atmosphere were out of the question.

At first these problems seemed insurmountable. But Alice kept their discussion moving by offering some possible solutions. They could pray together in the morning, she said, if both she and Gary would forgo Letterman and Leno at night. Gary said okay, but what about the morning craziness around this place? Alice promised to get the kids up and dressed half an hour earlier than usual. She said it would be her job to have them in the living room, ready and waiting for prayer, 20 minutes before Gary left for work. This sounded workable.

But they both knew that a few minutes of prayer in the morning was not enough time to provide the spiritual direction their children needed. How could they buy some more time in the evening? As they continued with their brainstorming, Alice came up with an idea: What if she took over the family finances—paying all the bills and balancing the checkbook. This would free up Gary's evenings so that he could lead the family in spiritual endeavors.

This sounded good, but then Gary noted another obstacle. "We can hardly make these kids sit still during dinner," he said. "How are we going to keep them at the table for another 15 minutes? And besides, they won't listen anyway. They want to get out and play."

After a few moments, Gary had an idea. "You know, we don't need to do devotions right after dinner," he said. "We could do them later in the evening, between 7:30 and 8:00, or maybe a half hour before the kids go to bed. And we don't need to do them at the kitchen table. We could gather in the family room, where the kids can cuddle up and be more comfortable."

One by one, possible solutions fell into place. Now they were ready for the final stage of the negotiation process.

Evaluate Options Objectively and Reasonably

The final step in the PAUSE principle is to take the ideas generated in the brainstorming session and evaluate them. Which of these ideas are realistic? Which ones are likely to work the best? What will it take to make them work? How can we cooperate to make this happen?

Even if the discussion has sailed smoothly up to this point, you may encounter difficulties when you start to evaluate ideas and try to agree on the best course of action. If the negotiation degenerates into a battle of wills, all you have done up to that point will be wasted. Therefore, it is crucial that you not rely on personal opinions in evaluating the options. Instead, try to use objective criteria.

As you seek to select the best solutions, you should try to discern and point out how different courses of action will benefit your spouse, your family, and other people in your lives. And if those benefits are not immediately visible, you should look for ways to test possible solutions to see if they are truly workable and beneficial.

The book of Daniel provides a profound example of a believer who confronts a seemingly insurmountable problem by thinking of a possible solution and arranging for that solution to be tested. Daniel and his friends had been taken captive to Babylon. As they prepared for service to the king, they were told that they must eat certain food, which was considered to be unclean according to Old Testament standards. It looked like they had two options: Either eat the food and offend God, or not eat the food and be killed for disobedience to the king.

With God's help, Daniel discerned the interests of the king and the official. The king probably wanted healthy and productive workers; the official wanted to keep his head. Rather than concentrating on his own interests, Daniel hunted for a solution that would satisfy both his interests *and* the Babylonians'. He suggested an objective test of his solution to the official: "Please test your servants for ten days: Give us nothing but vegetables to eat and water to drink. Then compare our appearance with that of the young men who eat the royal food, and treat your servants in accordance with what you see" (Daniel 1:12-13). At the end of the testing period 10 days later, the official had concrete evidence that Daniel's diet was healthier than what the king provided. "So the guard took away their choice food and the wine they were to drink and gave them vegetables instead" (v. 16).

In addition to seeking objective evaluations of possible solutions, continue to use all of the communication skills we discussed earlier in this book. Listen carefully to your spouse's suggestions; ask clarifying questions; show respect for his or her interests. Try to see things from his or her perspective, and when you offer a suggestion, ask for your spouse's feedback. And if your partner gets defensive or digs in his or her heels, move the discussion back to objective principles.

This type of evaluation strategy proved to be a key in securing an agreement between Gary and Alice. Through their discussion, they had come up with a few possible ways for their family to have more consistent devotions and prayer together. But since Gary had tried and failed so many times before, he was hesitant to set himself up for another embarrassing failure. When Alice saw that he was about to back off from making a commitment, she asked God to help her suggest a way that they could test their ideas in a manner that did not threaten Gary. By God's grace, she realized that if they sought to do something too ambitious, Gary might not even give it a try.

Therefore, Alice suggested a limited test period for the devotions (just as Daniel did with the Babylonians). For the next month they would have evening devotions just three times a week (instead of every night), in sessions of 15 minutes each. Gary could decide which nights worked best for him, and Alice and the kids would accommodate his schedule. After a month, they would sit down and assess how the program was working, fine-tune their efforts, or even come up with another possible way to allow Gary to assume his role as spiritual leader of the family while balancing the other pressures in his life.

Alice's suggestion was so reasonable that Gary felt comfortable giving it a try. Once they got started, Alice looked for every opportunity to thank Gary for his efforts. She hoped this positive reinforcement would spur him on as he sought to change his long-term habits.

By using the PAUSE principle, Alice and Gary turned a perennial conflict into an opportunity to understand and look out for each other's interests and to model cooperative negotiation to their children. And what was the bottom line? God was glorified, they served each other and their children, and they all took a small step forward in the process of being conformed to the image of Christ.

AS YOU GROW

If you are presently involved in a conflict, these questions will help you to apply the principles presented in this chapter.

1. How do you tend to negotiate: competitively (seeking primarily to get your own way) or cooperatively (looking out for others' interests as well as your own)?

2. How can you prepare to negotiate a reasonable agreement in your present situation?

3. How can you affirm your concern and respect for your spouse?

4. Seek to understand the interests of both you and your spouse by answering these questions:
     a. Which issues need to be resolved in order to settle this conflict? What positions have you and your spouse already taken on these issues?
     b. What are your interests in this situation?
     c. What are your spouse's interests in this situation?

5. What are some creative solutions or options that would satisfy as many interests as possible?

6. What are some ways that these options can be evaluated objectively and reasonably?

7. Go on record with the Lord by writing a prayer based on the principles taught in this chapter.

DIGGING DEEPER

Chapter 11 of *The Peacemaker: A Biblical Guide to Resolving Personal Conflict* provides additional guidance and practical examples on how to apply the PAUSE principle to negotiate substantive issues in your family, church, and place of work.

Part 3

FAMILY CONFLICT

■ ■ ■

8

Teaching Children to Be Peacemakers

When her seven-year-old twins, Ashley and Timmy, developed an interest in board games, Sandy hailed it as the greatest boon to domestic harmony since the invention of the two-bathroom house. She even trotted out and purchased all the usual staples for her kids: Monopoly, Parcheesi, Sorry!, Clue. She dreamed of her darlings consuming entire afternoons curled up on the living room floor tranquilly pushing their tokens around the game boards and, not incidentally, freeing her to get loads of housework done and maybe even some reading.

But it didn't happen that way. For the problem with board games is, you need two to play them. And her kids argued about what game they would play, who would go first, whose turn it was, who was cheating, and who would put the game away. Every seven and a half minutes she found herself standing over them, hands on hips, yelling, "Can't you kids ever play *nice*?" And that was on a good day.

She even considered hiding the games on the top shelf of a closet somewhere, but that wouldn't really solve anything. For if it wasn't board games, it was TV; if it wasn't TV, it was videos; if it wasn't videos, it was computer games; if it wasn't computer games, it was toys. And it seemed impossible for the twins to be at peace even when they were apart. If Ashley was playing computer games by herself, Timmy would suddenly get the urge to play computer games as well—right now!—and he wanted to play *his* games, not Ashley's. And vice versa. If there was anything to fight over, Sandy's kids would find a way to do it.

They fought over who would set the table before dinner, and who would dry and who would put away dishes after. They fought over who would walk the dog and who would feed the fish. They argued at the dinner table, always quick to criticize each other's table manners; and board up the windows if perchance one kid's dessert was slightly larger than the other's. Ashley would ride off on Timmy's skateboard without permission; Timmy would raise a ruckus, then he'd run off with a couple of Ashley's CDs, also without permission. It was tough enough for Sandy even to get a straight story out of either of them, much less solve the conflict.

But when Kent returned from work, oh, then it was a different story. Invariably, the kids dropped what they were doing—and suspended the argument in progress—to sprint to the front door and excitedly latch on to their daddy's legs, begging him to play with them. And also invariably, he was quick to comply.

And when Sandy brought up the kids' daytime behavior—"The kids were absolute brats today, Kent"—he could never see it.

"These kids? Brats?"

Sometimes Sandy and Kent even went at it in front of their children. She implored her husband for help in raising the kids and lambasted him for never taking her side. He took a classic see-no-evil, hear-no-evil approach.

The result was that nothing ever got solved, and some problems even got larger. For Sandy, each day was as bad as the last one—or worse.

■ ■ ■

Whoever first said raising children is a challenge should be inducted into the Understatement Hall of Fame. Children offer their parents continuous—and bountiful—blessing, true. They can be the picture of innocence, little independent units of humanity with bright, sparkling eyes and completely candid emotions. And when brought up to trust and love their Lord, they gladden many a parental heart.

But they, like the rest of us, were born into sin. And, as sinners, their hearts and minds are naturally inclined toward evil. This propensity toward sin plays itself out in many areas of kids' lives, but one of the more frequent is the one exhibited in our opening illustration.

Ashley and Timmy were fully caught up in sibling rivalry. Their major source of contention was who would get his or her way, who would control the other. And not only was it a problem within their four walls, but this behavior spread into the neighborhood as well. Ashley, for example, alienated many of her friends by continually imposing her will on them, by trying to control them.

All this takes its toll on Sandy, because she spends the majority of her day dealing with her kids' bickering. If she's not throwing up her hands in despair at their behavior now, she's worried that Ashley, in particular, may suffer in the future. She's concerned that her daughter may not be able to make or hold future relationships, that she may end up lonely and isolated.

Sandy ends each day feeling tired, angry, frustrated, and filled with self-doubt. Often she thinks she is a lousy mom because her children do not get along better with each other and with others.

MAKING LITTLE PEACEMAKERS

Jesus put Christian behavior in proper perspective when He was asked to identify the most important commandment. He said, "'Love the Lord your God with all your heart and with all your soul and with all your mind.' This is the first and greatest commandment." But then He added the second greatest: "'Love your neighbor as yourself'" (Matthew 22:37-39).

We can show our love for God through public worship, daily times of prayer and Bible study, and by giving to ministries that advance His kingdom. But He also calls us to demonstrate our love for Him by loving other people in concrete ways: "He has given us this command: Whoever loves God must also love his brother" (1 John 4:21). In a fallen world, such love for others does not come naturally. Nobody has to teach us to put "me" first; we do not need instruction on how to be selfish. And, if you didn't know it before you had children, you certainly know it after: *Nobody has to teach kids to fight.*

Love for other human beings is a gift of God, given primarily through the gracious work of the Holy Spirit, who changes our hearts and gives us a growing desire and ability to love other people (see Philippians 2:13). But God has also chosen to involve people, especially parents, in this educational process, using us to model and teach how to love one another.

This fact has a profound effect on how we raise our children. For the truth is, we must, with God's help, *teach* our children to respect others, live with others, and most importantly, love others. If they are to live lives pleasing to God, they will need education in how to get along with their siblings and friends. And to do this, they must know how to properly resolve conflicts even amongst themselves. In short, they must be taught peacemaking.

And we, their parents, must be the teachers. Our churches and schools may contribute to this goal, but when it comes to instructing our children in getting along with others, in resolving conflicts amongst themselves, parents must assume the primary responsibility to model and teach how to love others as God commands (see 1 John 3:23; Deuteronomy 6:6-7; Ephesians 6:4).

To fulfill this important responsibility, parents must learn to see this matter as God sees it. Through Scripture, God teaches us that relationships invariably involve conflict. He also teaches that we should be prepared to respond to these conflicts in a variety of constructive ways.

Some conflicts call for friendly discussion, teaching, or respectful debate (see John 3:1-21; 2 Timothy 2:24-26). In other situations we should overlook offenses, lay down rights, and do good to those who wrong us (see Luke 6:27-28; 9:51-56; Matthew 17:24-27). Sometimes love requires gentle confrontation or a firm rebuke (see John 4:1-42; Matthew 23:13-29). Above all, we need to be willing to forgive others just as in Christ God forgave us (see Luke 23:34; Ephesians 4:32).

As these passages indicate, getting along with other people requires a loving heart and a wide array of conflict resolution skills. In other words, it requires peacemaking.

Equipping Children for Life

Since all of life involves relationships and all relationships are prone to conflict, peacemaking is a key to success in life. This is as true for our children as it is for us. Therefore, the first requirement for teaching children to be peacemakers is to show that peacemaking skills are necessary if they want to succeed in their Christian life.

Peacemaking skills are especially important for any Christian who wants to be faithful to Christ in our increasingly godless culture. Consider Daniel and Esther, who lived in cultures that were completely hostile to their faith. Even when they faced life-or-death conflicts, they never compromised their spiritual integrity or commitment to God. They trusted in God and practiced some of the shrewdest conflict resolution found in Scripture. Amazingly, they not only survived, but they thrived as God blessed their efforts and moved them to pinnacles of influence in their societies. If our children learn these same skills at a young age, they too may be used of God in places of ministry or for political or corporate influence beyond our imaginations.

Kids need to learn that peacemaking is essential to their Christian witness. Jesus said, "By this all men will know that you are my disciples, if you love one another" (John 13:35). If our children are at odds with those around them, their attempts to witness will be fruitless. But if they learn how to love and be reconciled with those who wrong them, others are more likely to believe them when they talk about the love and forgiveness of God (John 17:23).

Peacemaking is also crucial for success in professional and vocational life. I have worked as a corporate engineer, a lawyer, and a ministry executive. I have hired, promoted, and fired people. These decisions were rarely based primarily on a person's technical skills. What I have valued most in an employee or manager is the ability to work as part of a team, to maintain strong relationships, and to build consensus so a group's gifts and energies stay focused on the project at hand. These are the skills of a peacemaker, and they are the same skills that will help your children succeed in the vocations to which God calls them.

Peacemaking is a key ingredient in a fulfilling marriage and a happy family (and a guard against divorce). Marriage brings two sinners into close proximity, where their selfish desires rub against each other day after day. Friction increases when God adds "little sinners" to the mix! There is only one way to deal with this volatile mixture: with humble confession, loving confrontation, and genuine forgiveness—the three basic tools of the biblical peacemaker.

In short, peacemaking equips children for life. If you want your children to glorify God, have fulfilling and enduring marriages, be fruitful in their careers, and contribute to their churches and the building of God's kingdom, teach them to be peacemakers!

Peacemaking Springs from Faith

As we mentioned earlier, peacemaking does not come naturally. Because of our sinful nature, we do not put our opponents' interests on the same level as our own, nor do we naturally seek resolutions to conflicts that benefit both parties. Like Timmy and Ashley in our opening story, our children are inclined to follow the sinful, selfish desires of their hearts that lead so often to conflict. This "me first" inclination is fed through a daily media barrage that exalts doing whatever it takes to get your own way, even if it involves violence or walking out on relational commitments. How can we stand against this tide and help our children to develop the character of a peacemaker?

To begin with, we must remember that the most important requirement of peacemaking is to understand who we are in Jesus Christ. Before the apostle Paul tells the Colossians what they should *do*, he reminds them of who they *are*: "*Therefore, as God's chosen people, holy and dearly loved*, clothe yourselves with compassion, kindness, humility, gentleness and patience" (Colossians 3:12, emphasis added).

A true peacemaker is guided, motivated, and empowered by his or her identity in Christ. This identity is based on faith in the most amazing promise we could ever hear: God has forgiven us all our sins and made peace with us through the death and resurrection of His Son (Romans 6:23; 1 Peter 3:18). And He has given us the freedom and power to turn from sin (and conflict), to be conformed to the likeness of Christ (Ephesians 1:18-20; Galatians 5:22-23; Romans 8:28-29), and to be His ambassadors of reconciliation (2 Corinthians 5:16-20).

It is the realization of who we are in Christ that enables us to do the unnatural work of dying to self, confessing sin, confronting in love, laying down rights, and forgiving deep hurts. Therefore, as you teach your children to be peacemakers, continually remind them to rejoice in who they are in Christ (forgiven and redeemed!) and in what He has done and promises to keep doing in and through them (see Philippians 4:4; 1:6).

Always Minister to Your Child's Heart

The second requirement of teaching children to be peacemakers is to help them understand the root cause of their conflicts. As we saw in chapter 2, James 4:1 provides a vital diagnostic tool: "What causes fights and quarrels among you? Don't they come from your desires that battle within you?"

Some of the desires that fuel our children's conflicts are clearly sinful, like pride, selfishness, jealousy, greed, or sibling rivalry. However, many of their conflicts will be generated by *good* desires elevated to *sinful demands*. For example, there is nothing inherently wrong with wanting to have a cookie or to watch a video or to spend more time with Dad or to excel in a school subject or sport. But if a child becomes resentful, sullen, or angry when not getting what he or she wants, it is evident that a worldly desire has taken control of his or her heart. In biblical terms, the desire has become a functional god or idol that is temporarily ruling that child's life.

Thus conflict becomes an X ray of our children's hearts. When others stand in the way of their desires and they quarrel and fight, their sinful desires are exposed. This gives us as parents an excellent opportunity to help our children break free from worldly desires.

But instead of beating them down with condemnation, we should pray for them and use questions, instruction, and gentle confrontation to help them see that something other than God is controlling their hearts and lives. At the same time, we should remind them of the forgiveness and freedom that God offers them through the gospel.

In our opening illustration, Sandy might want to take her children aside one at a time when an argument starts and, through gentle questions, help them examine their hearts and identify the desires that they have turned into demands or idols. (See the next chapter for tips on how to do this.) She should help them to see that they are being ruled by something other than God, which offends Him and will make their lives miserable. The goal of this part of the conversation is for the child to confess and renounce his or her sin.

Once the confession has been made, Sandy would turn to the gospel, ministering to her child's heart by emphasizing Jesus' forgiveness of that sin and His help in allowing her child to get along with his or her sibling. Jesus offers both forgiveness for the sin and the freedom to avoid fighting in the future.

This will not be a onetime process. The same controlling desires will beset our children's hearts and cause conflicts again and again, as they do ours. But as we repeatedly pray for them and guide them to examine their hearts, renounce their sin, and ask God for forgiveness and grace to change, they can experience a growing freedom from sin and deliverance from conflict (Romans 7:24-25).

Peacemaking Instruction

The third requirement for learning to be a peacemaker is deliberate, systematic instruction. Unfortunately, few children receive adequate instruction in peacemaking. The world rarely teaches it. When schools attempt to address the topic, they usually neglect the most important aspects of peacemaking, such as dealing with the heart. And even when we parents instruct our kids thoroughly in the general principles of the Christian faith, we often fail to concentrate specifically on teaching them to resolve personal conflict.

For example, we usually tell our children that they should confess their wrongs and forgive others. But we often leave them ignorant on *how* to do so in a biblical manner. Therefore, what we often hear from them is a grudging "I'm sorry" or a superficial "That's okay," both of which fail to convey genuine repentance or bring about reconciliation. This ignorance often carries into adulthood, where it is manifested in strained and broken marriages, church divisions, and needless lawsuits.

In Deuteronomy 6:7-9, God tells us to fight ignorance with diligent instruction: "Impress [God's commandments] on your children. Talk about them when you sit at home and when you walk along the road, when you lie down and when you get up. Tie them as symbols on your hands and bind them on your foreheads. Write them on the door frames of your houses and on your gates." This passage indicates that we should weave spiritual instruction, including peacemaking, into every aspect of daily life. This can be done in three ways.

Your Example Is a Great Teacher

After speaking to Christian parents at a conference, I was approached by a woman who was desperately seeking help on how to teach her children to deal with conflict in a constructive manner. For several minutes she described the many different conflicts that her four grade-school-age children engaged in on a daily basis. Then she asked what she could do to change these patterns. I asked her a question she didn't expect: "How do you and your husband deal with conflict?"

Tears welled up in her eyes and she hung her head in shame. "Oh, we're so awful," she said. "We are all over the slippery slope you described. We deny problems for a long time, and then things explode in a big argument. We talk and yell, but we never come to any real solutions. My greatest fear is that our children will grow up to be just like us."

I gently reminded her of a key principle of peacemaking: *It's never too late to start doing what is right.* Then I began to encourage her on how she and her husband could work together to turn things around in their family, especially by setting a better example of peacemaking themselves.

I reminded her that teaching by example is one of the most effective and highly commended instructional methods found in Scripture (see, for example, 1 Timothy 4:12, 15; 1 Corinthians 11:1; 1 Peter 2:21). Regardless of what you say to your children, most of what they learn about getting along with other people will come from what they see you do. If you live in denial or flee from conflict, your children will learn to become avoiders. If you lash out with angry words and blame others for everything that goes wrong, they will learn to become attackers. And if you refuse to forgive, they will learn how to be lonely and bitter people.

The reverse is also true. If your children see you humbly confess your sins and seek to change with God's help, they'll learn to become responsible, growing people. If they see you confront others in love, they'll learn to use their words to build up, not to destroy. And if they see you forgive those who have hurt you deeply, they'll learn to preserve relationships and model the gospel of Jesus Christ.

If you yourself have never learned how to deal with conflict biblically, do not despair. What I told the woman at the conference applies to all of us: *It's never too late to start doing what is right.* As you remember what Christ has done for you, and as you trust in His peacemaking promises and seek to learn and practice the biblical peacemaking principles we have discussed in this book, your children can have a steadily growing example of how to be peacemakers.

In the next chapter we will discuss several examples of how parents can model peacemaking while at the same time resolving conflict with their own children.

Instructional How-to's

Like any academic subject or artistic skill, learning peacemaking requires deliberate, systematic instruction; that is, it requires presenting the major conflict resolution principles of Scripture in a thorough, well-organized framework.

One of the most effective vehicles for this is *The Young Peacemaker*, which was mentioned in chapter 6. It is a 200-page children's curriculum written by my wife, Corlette, that is accompanied by 12 student activity books. This richly illustrated material quickly captures the interest and imagination of children and provides them with a thorough, systematic, and easy-to-remember process for resolving conflict.

An excellent way to teach this material is during family devotions. I especially encourage dads to take the initiative in leading this study. Each lesson involves a realistic conflict story, which children are usually happy to role-play. (The more dramatic your children are, the more interesting the discussion will be!)

After the role play, you can read and apply Bible passages that show your children how to identify the sinful desires that caused the conflict and resolve the problem in a way that honors God and restores relationships. One of the best ways to motivate them to study the material thoroughly is to allow the older children to lead a family study on a particular chapter or section. Allowing them to ask questions and suggest role plays, which Mom and Dad have to participate in, gives them a sense of responsibility that often motivates them to take the material even more seriously.

Appendix B provides a summary of the key principles taught in *The Young Peacemaker*, as well as information on how to order this material.

Use the Conflicts of Daily Life

Most families encounter conflict repeatedly every day. Kids find issues to fight over, whether it's who gets the last cookie or whose piece of toast has more butter on it. They are also extremely creative in finding ways to evade your instructions and neglect their chores or homework. That's the bad news. The good news is: Every one of these incidents offers a rich opportunity to help your children face their selfish desires and practice the basic principles of peacemaking.

On those wonderful (if rare) days when your family is living in peace, you can still find conflicts to discuss. Most stories and books your children read will involve conflict. The same is true of every television program and movie they watch.

My wife and I use simple questions at the right time to stimulate discussions. "Is the main character in this book using an escape response or an attack response?" "Is he acting wisely?" "What desires in his heart seem to have turned into idols?" "What consequences do you think he will experience if he gives in to those desires?" Or you might ask, "If you were the girl in this movie, how would you confess to her mother?" "If you were her mother, what would you say to show that you had really forgiven her?"

To reinforce your verbal instruction, use visual cues and reminders as taught in Deuteronomy 6:8-9. Also, *The Young Peacemaker* presents the key principles of peacemaking through cartoons, symbols, and diagrams. The artwork is reproducible, and your children can color it and post it in their bedrooms, on the refrigerator, or in other conspicuous places in your home or classroom. A quick glance at the "slippery slope of conflict" or "blame game" diagrams is often enough to remind a child of a key biblical principle that can avert a thoughtless conflict.

Practice, Practice, Practice

The fourth requirement for teaching children to be peacemakers is to provide them with a variety of appropriate social interactions so they can practice getting along with others in the midst of struggles and conflicts (see James 1:3-4; Romans 5:3-4; Philippians 4:9; Hebrews 5:14). This does not mean constantly surrounding your child with crowds of other kids. In fact, Scripture and experience both teach us that indiscriminate interaction with other people, especially at a young age, tends to aggravate bad habits, prolong immaturity, and result in grief (see Proverbs 1:8-33; 5:1-14; 7:1-27; 1 Corinthians 15:33).

What it means is that you should arrange for your children to interact with a variety of people suitable to their age and maturity, who will occasionally give them opportunities to experience conflict and practice peacemaking. This is an essential step in bringing children to maturity. By facing the sin in their hearts and working through conflict under their parents' guidance, they will be better prepared to deal responsibly with the conflicts they will inevitably face as they grow up and leave home.

Such situations abound, especially if we take advantage of opportunities to relate to people of all ages and stages in life. Church, sports, and artistic activities provide a good start. School activities, educational co-ops, and field trips allow further opportunities for social interaction.

Even greater blessings can be received as we obey the Bible's commands to practice hospitality and evangelism and serve those in need. This can involve ministry to the poor or disadvantaged, racial reconciliation work, and outreach to widows, the elderly, or single parents and their children. For added practice in relating to others (and resolving conflicts), ask other families to join you in some of these projects. Any family that brings the outside world to its dinner table, serves those in need, and colabors with other believing families will generally do very well teaching their kids to get along with others.

WHEN SHOULD YOU BEGIN?

I hear this question all the time. And I always offer the same answer: Begin teaching your children to be peacemakers as soon as they begin to get into conflict. For most children, that's pretty early!

Corlette and I began to teach Megan and Jeff the basic principles of peacemaking as soon as they could speak. Obviously, they couldn't cover every step in the Five A's of Confession (an abridged, children's version of the Seven A's), but we were surprised at how early they were hitting the main points of confession.

For example, when Jeff had just turned three, he got into a fight with his sister over which book they wanted Corlette to read to them. When Jeff didn't get his way, he lost his temper and hit his sister. Corlette took him into another room to administer discipline. She began by asking him some questions to help him understand what he had done wrong. The Lord quickly softened his heart, and Corlette was so impressed by the sincerity of his confession that she decided to exercise mercy and not give him the consequence they both knew he deserved.

After telling him that, she asked him to pray to the Lord about what he had done. Here is what this little three-year-old prayed: "Jesus, please forgive me for my selfish heart and fussy temper. Help me read the book Megan wants about the rabbit. And thank You, Jesus, that Mommy not spank me this time. In Jesus' name, Amen."

Although Jeff had not hit all the Five A's, he covered the major points: He went to the root of the problem and specifically admitted the idolatrous heart condition that moved him to hurt his sister when he did not get his way. He indicated how he needed to alter his choices in the future. And he implicitly accepted the consequences that his sin deserved. If more adults made this kind of confession, my work as a professional conciliator would go much more smoothly!

Another common question that many parents wrestle with is whether they should require a child to make a confession when he or she does not seem to be truly repentant. Opinions will differ, but I'll share what Corlette and I did.

As soon as our children could speak, we required them to make a confession whenever they did something wrong. (In most cases, we first talked and prayed with them to help them understand how they had disobeyed God's commands.) Even though they were obviously not sincere some of the time, we believed that it would be good for them to develop the habit of at least saying the right words. (Many adults do not have the foggiest idea how to make a good confession; at least our children would not be able to plead ignorance!)

One day, when Megan was about five, we decided it was time to change the ground rules for her. She and her mother had had a conflict, and Corlette was requiring Megan to admit what she had done wrong.

As I listened from the other room, I was troubled by how insincere Megan seemed to be. I walked into the room and interrupted her confession. "Megan," I said, "you obviously don't mean the words you are saying. You are old enough now that you should mean what you say. Otherwise you are not being a truth-speaker. Please go up to your room and think and pray about what has happened, and do not come down until you can sincerely confess what you did wrong."

Megan headed toward her room with a cold and sullen look on her face, leaving Corlette and me in the kitchen wondering if this were the right move to make. (Parenting is filled with so much self-doubt, I thank God I have a partner to share these tough times with.) We sat there and prayed that God would reach through to our daughter's hard heart and help her to see how selfishly she had been acting.

About 10 minutes later, we heard Megan's steps on the stairs and turned to face her. I could tell from her countenance that her heart had changed. Instead of the cold, defiant look, there was a softness in her eyes as she walked quickly to Corlette, threw her arms around her mother, and gave a heartfelt confession. The two were reconciled amidst a wave of tears.

This marked a new season in Megan's life, which Jeff entered a short time later as well. Once we concluded that they were mature enough to understand and take responsibility for their actions, we did all we could to encourage them to make sincere confessions, even if it meant long talks and prayer together, or having them sit alone to think about their actions.

Our resolve to teach and instruct, and then leave room for the Holy Spirit to act, was strengthened when we read Paul's instructions in 2 Timothy 2:24-25: "And the Lord's servant must not quarrel; instead, he must be kind to everyone, able to teach, not resentful. Those who oppose him he must gently instruct [and this is where our job ends and God's begins], in the hope that God will grant them repentance leading them to a knowledge of the truth."

Of course, our children's confessions seem less than sincere at times (as do ours, I'm sorry to say). But as all four of us gain a deeper understanding of God's amazing grace and forgiveness for us, there is a noticeable improvement in our ability to genuinely grieve over our sins against one another, to confess our wrongs from the heart, and to sincerely rejoice in God's marvelous gift of reconciliation.

IT'S NEVER TOO LATE

Many parents also ask me how to teach peacemaking to older children who have had many years to develop terrible conflict resolution skills. Often these habits are so ingrained and relationships so damaged that the situation seems beyond hope. But remember what we identified earlier as a key peacemaking principle: *It's never too late to start doing what is right.*

If you have neglected to teach your children how to respond to conflict biblically (and especially if you have failed to model these principles), the starting point is to come clean to God and to them. Confess your failure to God and ask for His forgiveness and for His healing and redeeming grace. Then call a family meeting, or meet privately with each child, and do a Seven-A confession regarding your failure.

Admit specifically your ignorance, laziness, or lack of faith or self-discipline. Apologize for the effect your failure has had on them. Point out the consequences of your failure, and help them see the consequences they are experiencing as they follow the same patterns.

Then explain how you are asking God to change things, and make a commitment to work with them, by God's grace, to develop new conflict resolution habits in your family. Finally, warn them that things will not change overnight, but that with God's help you can all change those bad habits and learn how to be peacemakers. (In the next chapter, we will discuss several specific ways you can make good on this commitment by practicing peacemaking in common conflicts with your children.)

If they are responsive to this approach, you can begin the teaching process as discussed above. If a child is resistant, unmoved, or unrepentant, you will have additional barriers to overcome. Modeling peacemaking and repenting of your own wrongs again and again will be essential. A resistant child will pick up on your failures more quickly than you and use them as a basis to accuse you of hypocrisy. Blame shifting or defensiveness on your part will not change that child's heart. The only way to deal with your own wrongs is through confession and repentance. Remember, "He who conceals his sins does not prosper, but whoever confesses and renounces them finds mercy" (Proverbs 28:13).

With some children you may be able to enlist the aid of another adult they trust to help them come to grips with their destructive habits for resolving conflict. This might be a church elder, youth pastor, teacher, relative, or close family friend.

In most cases this educational process will also require repeated efforts to help your child see the consequences of his or her bad choices. As you make these efforts, take great care to practice gentleness and humility. Instead of rubbing your child's nose in his or her mistakes, gently admit how your choices have created similar consequences. (You want to create an environment where instead of trying to hide his or her problems, your child will feel safe in coming to you for help.) In some cases you may have to resist the temptation to rescue your child from his or her problems and instead let him or her experience the natural consequences of foolish choices. As Scripture promises, "A hot-tempered man must pay the penalty; if you rescue him, you will have to do it again" (Proverbs 19:19).

In most cases this learning process will take time. You will need to cover the same ground again and again. Here again, Paul's exhortation to Timothy is essential: Your job is to gently instruct as you also pray fervently that the Holy Spirit will grant your child repentance.

IT IS WORTH THE EFFORT

Teaching children to be peacemakers is one of the most challenging responsibilities of being a parent. It requires faith and reliance on God, ministry to our children's hearts, systematic instruction, and careful guidance of their social involvement.

The results of this labor are well worth the effort, however. By continually reminding our children of who they are in Christ, we can inspire them to imitate His love, renounce sinful desires, and respond to conflict in a way that honors Him. This faith and behavior can help to deepen their Christian witness, preserve their friendships, strengthen their marriages, and give them greater success in the workplace.

As our children are transformed by God and learn to love others as they love themselves, even in the midst of conflict, they will develop the worshiping hearts and serving hands that God delights to use to build His kingdom.

What a privilege it is for parents to participate in this process!

May we be faithful to this call by consistently teaching and modeling biblical peacemaking in every aspect of our homes and lives.

AS YOU GROW

1. The most important way to teach your children to be peacemakers is through your own example. If you have not set a good example so far, confess that to your children, specifically describing how you have failed to deal with conflict in a way that honors God. Ask for your children's prayers as you seek to grow in the days ahead. Your example of humility will set the stage for how they need to face their weaknesses as peacemakers.

2. Teaching children to be peacemakers requires dedication, patience, and perseverance. Here are the key steps you will need to repeat day after day as God works in their lives.
   a. Remind them regularly of who they are in Christ: forgiven and redeemed!
   b. Minister to their hearts, seeking to help them identify and renounce the idols (desires-turned-into-demands) that may rule their hearts.
   c. Provide regular, systematic instruction, primarily by your example, but also by teaching through *The Young Peacemaker* every year or two, and by using stories, movies, and the normal conflicts of family life as teaching opportunities.
   d. Provide your children with opportunities for social interactions where conflicts can arise and you can help them practice peacemaking skills.

3. If your children are older and have developed sinful conflict resolution habits, do not give up. It's never too late to start doing what is right! Confess where you have failed to model and teach peacemaking, and explain how you plan to help your whole family grow in this area. Start to teach and discuss the principles in this chapter one at a time, realizing that change will not come easily or quickly. If your child refuses to respond, look for help from other families or a youth pastor in your church. Most of all, pray, pray, pray, remembering God's promise to be a God to you and to your children forever!

DIGGING DEEPER

For further guidance on how to reach your children's hearts and teach them how to be peacemakers, see:

- *The Young Peacemaker,* by Corlette Sande
- *Shepherding a Child's Heart,* by Tedd Tripp
- *Parenting Isn't for Cowards,* by Dr. James Dobson

9

Making Peace with Children

The laboratory that is day-to-day life will give your children many—you might think *way too many*—opportunities to put into practice the peacemaking principles you want to instill in them. Conflict, like trouble, is inevitable—"as surely as sparks fly upward," as Job observed (Job 5:7)—and kids just being kids will quarrel and fight. But with God's help and guidance, and your systematic instruction, they can truly learn to resolve conflicts themselves in a peaceable and God-honoring way.

But what about *your* run-ins with your kids? They will inevitably push against the boundaries and stretch the limits of your parental supervision and guidance. They are, after all, independent persons, with minds and wills of their own, and in their struggle for autonomy they often test your authority. What results are conflicts between children and their parents.

Take the case of Jessica, for example. Jessica is 14, very independent, and what her parents in their more diplomatic moods call a "strong-willed child." She bops into the kitchen one Saturday with the lyrics from the newest boy-band release bombarding her ears and pulls the headset from her portable CD player down to her neck long enough to announce: "I'm going to the mall."

Mom places the rubber spatula on the counter—Saturday is baking day—and gives her daughter the once-over. "In that?"

"Well ... *yeah*."

"Why don't you wear one of those outfits Aunt Marsha gave you for Christmas, Jess? The one with the swan on it."

"*Mo-o-om.*" Jessica folds her arms.

"You know your father and I don't like that outfit," Mom says. "It's so ... small."

"Mel and Lex will be wearing outfits *just like this*, and they don't get hassled all the time by their parents."

"You're going with Melody and Alexis?"

"And Thor."

"Thor too?"

"*Hello-o-o-o!*" Jessica looks at the ceiling. "Where Mel goes, Thor goes too."

In walks Dad, sweat streaming off his temples. "Those people in Arizona have it figured out," he proclaims. "Dump 12 tons of rocks on your lawn. Put the lawnmower away for..."—he swivels his head—"where's she going?"

"Mall," Mom says. She picks up the spatula and starts evening out the frosting on the brownies. "With Thor."

Jessica unfolds her arms, stomps to the sofa, throws herself into the corner of it, and refolds her arms. "I knew it," she says. "I knew this would turn into a big production."

"What for?" Dad asks Mom.

She points the spatula toward Jessica. "Ask your daughter."

"What for?" Dad asks Jessica.

"To see a movie and buy CDs," Jessica answers.

"What movie? What CDs?" Dad perches himself on the edge of the recliner, facing the couch.

"Don't know yet. Don't know yet."

Mom walks over to the recliner. "Thor gets them into R-rated movies," she says.

Jessica snorts. "*Not even!*"

"Jess," Dad says, leaning forward and propping his elbows on his quads, "you know we're concerned about your friends and what you do with them when you go to the mall."

"Oh, great." Jessica rolls her eyes. "*This* again."

Mom sits on the arm of the recliner. "It's just that a lot of movies preach against Christian virtues. And the music you listen to has lots of sex and drugs in it."

"Cassette number 72," Jessica says. "Friends, movies, music. Call now. 1-800-NAG-NAG. Operators are standing by."

"That'll be enough, young lady," Dad interjects.

"Can I go now?"

Then Mom, more reasoned: "Jess, honey, we just don't want you to ruin your life like ... like..."

"Like Thor?"

"Like a lot of kids." Mom takes a breath. "We want you to grow up following the Lord. You know that."

"Can I go now?"

"I don't think so," Dad says.

Jessica bolts to her feet. "Look!" she says. "I'm telling you where I'm going, who I'm going with, and what we're going to do. You're getting way more out of me than Mel and Lex's parents do!"

Dad is on his feet now too. He points a finger. "I said, that'll be enough!"

"I can't do anything around this place!" Jessica is shouting now.

"Don't you raise your voice to me!"

"I'm living with Nazis." Jessica throws herself back onto the couch.

"Oh, so we're Nazis now." Dad goes very in-your-face. By now he's leaning over the couch. "We feed you. We clothe you. We buy you everything your little heart desires. And we're *Nazis*?"

"Honey," Mom counsels.

"Until you're 18, young lady, you're living in our house, and you'll follow our rules."

"Nazi!"

"You might change your mind about us being Nazis once you get to juvenile hall."

"I can't be 18 soon enough!"

"And if you think you're getting your driver's license when you turn 16, you'd better think again."

Jessica jumps to her feet and starts for the stairs. Halfway up the stairs she turns. "I hate you!" she screams. She stomps up the rest of the way and turns again. "I hate you!"

■ ■ ■

The teenage years. It's a time for changes, challenges, and conflicts. But children do not instantly become rebellious the moment they lean over and blow out 13 candles on their birthday cake. Even before they can walk, children are kicking against the goads of parental authority.

And for us parents, who have been there, done that, and have, because of our own youthful mischief, a heightened appreciation of strong parental discipline and firm boundaries, it is easy to become frustrated and angry with a rebellious child.

APPLYING THE FOUR G'S
Thankfully, through the Scriptures God has provided parents with effective principles for resolving conflict with our teens. We can find help during these challenging times by applying the Four G's of conflict resolution to our relationships with our children.

Glorify God, Not Sinful Behavior
A lot of our frustration with our children emanates from a less-than-noble source: the effect our children's behavior has on our comfort and convenience. Our kids' sinful acts make our own lives less relaxed, less peaceful, and more hectic. Or perhaps we take the misbehavior personally. It makes us look bad—maybe even incompetent as parents. And by golly, we aren't going to let a mere child, one under our authority, do *that*. We control the kid, not the kid us.

This was Jessica's parents' motivation. And their daughter's sinful behavior had repeated itself so often, they were increasingly inclined to become angry and even bitter toward her.

If they're not careful, they will begin to "glorify" Jessica's behavior; that is, become consumed by thoughts of how wrong she is and how unfair it is for her to be so contrary and willful. But as they dwell on her behavior, they inevitably take their focus off the Lord. In doing so, they cease to glorify Him as they should.

The fact is, every time we have a conflict with a child, we have a choice to make: Am I going to make much of my child's sin, or am I going to make much of God's redeeming grace? It's one or the other. We will either "glorify" our child, or we will glorify the Lord.

The more you focus on your child's behavior, the more likely you are to be controlled by bitterness, resentment, or anger. The more you focus on God's love and promises, the more likely you are to be led to repent, confess, forgive, and change.

Therefore, when you find yourself in a conflict with your child, develop the habit of pausing for a moment before you speak. Reflect on who you are in Christ—redeemed and forgiven—and remember that God's covenant is not only for you but for your child as well (Acts 2:39). Quietly thank God for all He has done for you and your child through Christ and for all He is presently doing for both of you through the Holy Spirit.

Indeed, the replacement principle, outlined in chapter 6, can be quite useful here. This mental exercise urges us to replace the negative thoughts we harbor about our child with positive ones. When we become obsessed with our child's behavior, we should ask for God's help and deliberately pray for our child or think of something about him or her that is, as the apostle Paul writes, true, noble, right, pure, lovely, admirable, excellent, or praiseworthy (Philippians 4:8).

Such reflection usually results in an increased sense of love for God and a renewed faith that He is always up to something good, even in the midst of conflict (see Romans 8:28-29). In short, God ensures that things work out for the good for those who love Him—and that they work out to His glory.

As Jesus taught in John 14:15, the more we love God, the more motivated we will be to obey His commands, many of which relate directly to peacemaking: Let your gentleness be evident to all. Let no unwholesome word come out of your mouth. Speak the truth in love. Forgive as God has forgiven you.

As you keep your heart centered on God, He will empower you to follow the peacemaking principles He has set forth in His Word. As you do so, it will be evident to those around you that something unusual is going on. In spite of the frustration and irritation you may feel toward your child, you are responding in a way that is not natural. This gives evidence that it is Christ working in you, which brings Him praise and glory.

Get the Log Out of Your Own Eye

My children, Megan and Jeff, had been squabbling with each other all week. They were constantly trying to control each other. "It's my turn to go first," "I get the last donut," "I want to watch this video, not that one," etc. Their constant bickering had worn Corlette down, and she had become irritable toward them and me.

On Sunday morning Corlette went to church early to help with choir. When the kids came out to get in the car a little later, they began to argue about who got to sit in the front seat. I was fed up with their behavior and lost my temper. "Be quiet!" I shouted. "Jeff, you get in the front seat, and Megan, you get in the back!"

But since my frustration had finally boiled over in anger, I didn't stop there. As I got into the car, I adjusted the rearview mirror so I could catch Megan's eye as she cowered in a corner of the backseat. As we drove to church, I sharply lectured both of them. Speaking in an unusually loud voice, I told them I was very angry with them for how they had been behaving, and I was going to make them very sorry for the grief they had been causing all week. When I paused to take a breath, Jeff timidly asked, "Is your anger rightful anger, Daddy?"

His words cut me to the heart. The Holy Spirit used his simple question to reveal the sinful anger that had been spilling out of my heart as we drove to church. I had allowed a good desire to become a controlling idol. I wanted my children to get along with each other. Although I had tried to convince myself that my motive was that I wanted them to honor God through right behavior, the overflowing anger in my heart showed that my primary motive was far more selfish: When they get along with each other, my wife is happier and my life is more peaceful, convenient, and comfortable. They were not fulfilling my desire, so I had used my tongue like a knife, wounding them to fulfill my idolatrous demand for an easy and pleasant life.

Deeply convicted, I pulled into a vacant parking lot and stopped the car. With tears in my eyes, I turned to my children and confessed my sin against them.

"I am so sorry for speaking to you the way I did. I let a good desire become a monster demand. I wanted you to get along with each other, but I wanted it for the wrong reasons. I wanted it so that my life would be easy and comfortable, and when you didn't do that, I became angry with you and hurt you with my words. It is very wrong of me to punish you for not serving my idols. My discipline should only be given to help you to obey and honor God. I know I scared and hurt both of you very much, and I am so sorry. With God's help, I'll try to never let my desire for peace and quiet cause me to lash out at you in anger. Will you please forgive me?"

Both of my children dissolved into tears. Throwing their arms around me, they lovingly said, "I forgive you, Daddy," and then quickly confessed their own sinful behavior against each other and against Corlette and me. We sat there for another 10 minutes, hugging, crying, and forgiving one another. We talked about the idolatrous desires that had been controlling our hearts, and each of us prayed for God to replace those desires with a greater love for Him.

As we drove on to church, each of us felt an exhilarating sense of peace and joy. God's redeeming grace had helped us to repent of our wrongs and experience a profound reconciliation. We were a few minutes late for church, but I have seldom sung praises to God with such an intense feeling of thankfulness and joy.

As this story illustrates, James 4:1-2 is often applicable to conflicts between parents and children: "What causes fights and quarrels among you? Don't they come from your desires that battle within you? You want something but don't get it. You kill and covet, but you cannot have what you want. You quarrel and fight. You do not have, because you do not ask God."

It is usually quite easy for parents to identify the desires that rule their children's hearts. The more important task is for us to identify the idols that are ruling our own hearts, which generally include a consuming desire for respect, appreciation, control, comfort, convenience, or, to put it in simple terms, peace and quiet. Whenever we find ourselves feeling frustrated, bitter, resentful, or angry toward our children, there is a good chance that we have elevated a desire for these good things to a sinful demand.

Therefore, whenever you are in a conflict with your child and feel strong negative emotions, stop the discussion and take a minute to go to the Lord in prayer. Ask Him to help you discern the desires that are ruling your heart. If you identify specific desires-elevated-to-demands, confess them to God and to your child, and ask the Lord to replace them with a stronger love for Him and a concern to see your child live a life that is honoring to God.

If you realize that your heart has overflowed in sinful words or actions, obey Jesus' command to get the plank out of your own eye before trying to remove the speck from your child's eye. Using the Seven A's of Confession (see chapter 4), set an example for your child by thoroughly confessing your wrongs. In many cases your confession will change the tone of your discussion and inspire your child to acknowledge his or her contribution to the problem. Even if the child doesn't respond that way, by deliberately renouncing the idols that ruled your heart, you will at least be able to see more clearly to remove the speck from your child's eye.

In some cases a child will try to use your sin and confession as a way to obscure or justify his or her own wrongs or lack of respect for your authority. When that happens, you will need to help the child see that God calls him or her to do what is right and to obey his or her parents even if they themselves fail to behave perfectly. Point out that God's commands to honor and obey parents are not conditioned on the parents' behavior (see Exodus 20:12; Ephesians 6:1-3; compare Matthew 23:1-3). Jesus commands children—and all of us, for that matter—to love their enemies, to do good to those who hate them, to bless those who curse them, and to pray for those who mistreat them (Luke 6:27). If so, how much more should the child respect and do good to his or her parents, even when they themselves have stumbled in some way.

The important thing to remember is that the most effective way to teach others is by example. When parents confess their wrong quickly, thoroughly, and without excuses, their children will usually learn to do the same. This will not always happen quickly or consistently, but as we provide a steady example of humble and biblical confession, we will usually see conflicts resolved more quickly and our children learning a skill that will benefit them and those around them throughout their lives.

Go and Show Your Brother His Fault, Always Ministering the Gospel

During my early years of parenting, I majored in "law giving." When my children misbehaved, I confronted them, pointed out what they had done wrong, administered a consequence, and told them how they should behave in the future. Although I usually ended the discussion by hugging them and praying with them, the overriding emphasis of my correction was on what they should or should not do. I was full of "should's" and "should not's." Like the ancient Israelites, my children knew what it was like to live "under the law."

As the story at the end of chapter 5 reveals, God used my wife to open my eyes to the need to minister both the law *and* the gospel to my children when confronting them. The law shows our children what *they should do.* The gospel reminds them of what *God has done and is doing.* Focusing on God's work in us is a vital part of confrontation because it injects hope into the situation and helps motivate our children to cooperate with His work in their lives.

For example, when confronting my daughter one day about her disrespectful attitude toward her mother, I did a thorough job of pointing out how she was disobeying God's command to honor her mother and making life unpleasant for the entire family. But then I realized that I had backed her into a corner without offering a way out—just as I had done at the mountain camp conference mentioned in chapter 5. Modeling Corlette's wonderful example at that conference, I extended the gospel to Megan.

"Honey," I said. "Today has not gone well for you or your mother. But it can start to get better right now. Jesus died for all the sin you committed today. He took it on His shoulders on the cross, and He paid the full penalty for it. He washed your guilt away with His own blood. And He is still working for you today. He wants to come into your heart in a fresh way to wash away the selfish, angry desires that led you to say the things you said to your mother."

Holding my cupped hands out to her, I continued. "He is holding out forgiveness to you right now, and He's offering you the power to turn away from your selfishness, confess your sin, and be reconciled to Mommy. It's a free gift. All you have to do is receive it."

At first Megan wouldn't look me in the eye, and as I held out my hands, she looked away. Her heart was hard, and I realized she needed time to think about what I had said. Before leaving the room, I gently asked her to look me in the eyes. When she did, I asked her if she could see the deep love that I felt for her. She searched my eyes for a moment, and gave a tentative nod. I said, "I love you very, very much. And Jesus loves you even more. Nothing you do will ever change that." As I left the room, I asked her to think about what I said, and told her I would be back in a few minutes.

I found Corlette, and together we prayed that God would graciously soften our daughter's hard heart. After about 10 minutes, I returned to Megan's room. Her face had softened somewhat, but she had not come completely out of her shell. She looked me in the eye to see if the look of love was still there. Sensing that she was still teetering on a fence between defiance and repentance, I assured her again of both Jesus' love and mine. She struggled internally for a few more moments, and then caved in. She jumped up and rushed into my arms. She confessed her sin, and we spent quite a bit of time talking and praying about the idols that had been controlling her heart for most of the morning. She accepted the consequences of her sin and received my forgiveness. She then wanted to find her mother, and the two of them walked through a similar time of confession and forgiveness.

Of course, we don't always see such a quick response in our children. On some days they will stubbornly dig themselves into a hole and refuse to come out for hours. But we have seen that the more consistently and clearly we hold out the gospel when confronting them, the more likely they are to let go of their pride and reach out for the gift of forgiveness.

In addition to providing hope for reconciliation, the gospel is an essential element in reaching our children's hearts and helping them to understand and deal with the desires and motivations that give rise to their actions. If all we talk about is the law, what they should and should not do, we will necessarily limit our discussion to their surface behavior, which will teach them to be superficial people. They will learn to put on whatever face or appearance they think will appease us, but their hearts will still be dominated by worldly desires that will rule them when they are not in our presence. In other words, we will teach them to be good little Pharisees, looking good on the outside but "full of dead men's bones" on the inside (Matthew 23:27).

But when we bring the gospel into the picture, we can move to a deeper level of discussion. We can remind them that Jesus came to deliver us not only from the penalty of sin, but also from its power. He does this by progressively changing our heart so that instead of constantly following our old selfish desires, we develop a growing desire to love and please God.

With this promise in mind, we should seek to draw our children out and help them to discern the sinful desires that have been ruling their hearts. These may include selfishness, pride, control, laziness, coveting, or a preoccupation with controlling others or gaining their approval. As our children come to see how these desires-turned-into-demands have been ruling their hearts, they will have the opportunity to confess and renounce them and to ask God to change their hearts so they have one controlling desire: to know God's love and respond to it with faith and obedience.

When confronting our children, we should also apply the principles discussed in chapter 5. Overlooking minor offenses, choosing an appropriate time and place to talk, listening to and seeking to understand their perspective, paraphrasing and clarifying, carefully choosing our words to build up and not tear down—all are key elements in an effective confrontation. The more we practice using these elements, the more constructive and productive our conversations are likely to be.

Go and Be Reconciled

It was Christmas vacation, and Mom was having a tough day with her 10-year-old daughter, Amy. First it was the Internet. Amy had logged on at 9:30 A.M. and e-mailed a few friends, then had run out of the house to play, forgetting to log off and free up the phone line. Mom thus missed an important call she was expecting at 10:00. She hunted for her daughter, found her at the neighbor's, bawled her out, and demanded an apology.

"I'm sorry, Mom," Amy said matter-of-factly.

Later in the morning Mom was carrying an armload of laundry from the dryer to her bedroom and tripped over one of Amy's toys, falling down and sending the laundry all over the hallway.

"Amy!" Mom shrieked.

The girl cracked her room door and poked a head through.

"I've told you a thousand times to put your Marvin the Martian stuff away!"

"Okay, Mom," she said, retreating into her room and closing the door, "Sorry," the last word uttered as the door closed.

Then there was a set-to over lunch dishes. Amy ate her sandwich and hustled back to her room without putting the dishes in the dishwasher, which was her assigned duty after lunch.

"Amy!" Mom called. "You forgot to put the dishes in the dishwasher."

"Okay, Mom," came the return call.

Ten minutes later the dishes were still on the table.

"Amy! Come here and take care of the dishes."

No reply this time.

"Amy! You get down here right now and do these dishes!"

This got Amy into the kitchen at any rate. And when she stomped in, Mom lectured her about obeying orders and fulfilling her duties around the house.

"Okay," Amy said. *"Okay!"*

"And I want you to apologize to me."

Amy sighed deeply. "Okay, Mom," she said. "I'm sorry." And she was immediately out of the room.

The last straw came in the middle of the afternoon, when Amy was dribbling her basketball around the front room. She bounced it hard once and it got away from her, landing on top of the piano, where it struck Mom's prized bust of Johann Sebastian Bach and sent it shattering to the floor.

Mom came running from the dining room. "Oh!" she shrieked, stooping to inspect the damage.

Amy grabbed her ball and clutched it to her chest.

Mom stood up, purpling with rage. "You know you are *not* to dribble your basketball in the house," she yelled. "Haven't I told you that?"

Amy nodded solemnly. "I'm sorry, Mom." Then she dropped to her knees and began picking up pieces of the bust. "Maybe we can glue it," she said.

"Stop!" Mom looked severely at her daughter. "I'll do it. Just leave, okay?"

"I'm sorry, Mom," Amy said.

Mom hoisted a forefinger toward the stairs. "Go!" she yelled. "Leave!"

"It was an accident, Mom," Amy said earnestly. "I didn't mean to break it."

"Just go!"

Amy paused. "Do you forgive me, Mom?"

Mom continued hunting down broken fragments of the bust.

"Mom?"

"Yeah, I forgive you," Mom said brusquely, still absorbed in damage assessment.

"But I don't feel like you've really forgiven me."

There are times when it is difficult to forgive a child. When they have hurt another person, violated our trust, damaged treasured possessions, drained our reserves of compassion through repeated wrongs, or seemed insincere in their confession, it is all too easy to make them pay by withholding our forgiveness.

But as we saw in chapter 6, withholding forgiveness is not an option for a Christian. In response to God's infinitely precious gift of forgiveness to us, we must offer the same kind of forgiveness to those who have wronged us (see Matthew 6:14-15; 18:21-32; Ephesians 4:32; Colossians 3:13).

So how do we overcome obstacles to forgiveness? If your son (or daughter) has not yet confessed to his sin, you need to lovingly confront him, as described in the previous section and in chapter 5, making every effort to help the child see the wrong in his actions.

If the child confesses but seems insincere, it is often appropriate to tell him so, and explain why it is hard to believe that he is really sorry for what he has done. In some cases it may be helpful to give the child a little while to think more about what he has done and then to make a more thoughtful confession.

But sometimes a child's lack of spiritual maturity will prevent him or her from mustering as much sincerity as we want. In those cases we need to remember that we ourselves often fall short of the deep, profound repentance that our sins call for, and yet God is incredibly compassionate and merciful with us. This realization should move us to treat our children likewise and to grant them forgiveness, even if the confession is less than perfect.

As God gives me grace to forgive my children, I make it a point to be sure that I have their complete attention. I look them in the eye and say, "I forgive you, just as God has forgiven me through Jesus." I then draw my children into my arms and whisper the children's version of the four promises of forgiveness in their ear: "Good thought, hurt you not, gossip never, friends forever." I give them a special hug as I say the last two words.

Through these verbal and physical cues, I try to send a clear, repeated message that when they confess their wrongs, they will find complete forgiveness from their father and a full restoration of our relationship. I want to tear down every obstacle that may make them hesitant to come to me when they do something wrong in the future. Offering total forgiveness will encourage them to confess future wrongs quickly, and also help model to them the incomparably great mercy and forgiveness they can expect from their heavenly Father.

Forgiveness means that our relationship with our children will be fully restored. We will not hold them at a distance or punish them by giving them the cold shoulder. But forgiveness does not mean that they will necessarily be freed from the natural consequences of their wrongs. For minor infractions, it is sometimes appropriate to be merciful and not impose consequences. But when they have committed a major wrong, it is often necessary to help them grow by experiencing appropriately related consequences (see Proverbs 19:19). This may involve applying corporal punishment, repairing or replacing damaged property (as the child is able), or the loss of privileges. Whatever the consequence, our goal should always be to help them learn to take responsibility for their actions and to turn from such behavior in the future.

Above all else, however, our goal in granting forgiveness should be to bring honor and praise to God by imitating the marvelous forgiveness He has given to us through His Son. When our children and those around us consistently witness this type of modeling, the gospel will be more credible, and they will be encouraged to offer the same type of forgiveness to those who have wronged them.

NATURAL NEGOTIATORS

One evening a windstorm blew a large branch off one of our trees. It fell on a neighbor's garage, pinning our power line beneath it. Fearing the power line would break and cause a fire, I scrambled to get a saw and ladder so I could quickly remove the branch. It took me about 30 minutes to complete the job.

When I came inside, I walked past my son's room and noticed he was not in bed as he should have been. I peeked in and saw Jeff standing on his toy box looking out the back window. Obviously, he had been watching me cut apart the branch. Although I realized that watching this project would have been nearly irresistible for a four-year-old boy, I was irritated that he had disobeyed our rule that he is to stay in bed. I quietly tiptoed up behind him and announced my presence by booming, "Jeffrey Charles Sande, what are you doing out of bed?"

Jeff pivoted, looked up at my looming figure, understood his jeopardy, and realized in an instant that he had to do some very quick negotiation. The wheels were spinning furiously in his little mind as he searched for a way to avoid the consequence of his disobedience. He knew instinctively that if he dwelt on *his interests*, he had little hope for mercy. Therefore he refrained from saying, "Daddy, I don't like going to bed so early and I wanted to watch you cut the tree apart."

Instead, even though he had never studied Philippians 2:4 ("Look not only to your own interests, but also to the interests of others"), he knew that his only hope was to appeal to something *I valued*. In less than three seconds, his eyes lit up as he found the key.

"Daddy," he said. "I was worried about you up on the roof. So I've been praying that Jesus would keep you from falling."

Bingo.

Jeff knew that Daddy values love and concern for others, as well as praying to Jesus for protection. Even though I knew this was probably not his primary reason for standing at the window, my heart warmed and my irritation dissipated. Remembering many other incidents when he had been deeply concerned about my well-being, I decided to give Jeff the benefit of the doubt and believe that he had prayed for my safety. So judgment gave way to mercy. Thanking him for his concern, I tucked him into bed, gave him a hug, and reminded him to stay there.

Walking out the door, I smiled to myself as I realized that children are natural negotiators. Since they are in a weaker power position than their parents and cannot simply dictate events, children learn that the best way to get what they want (or avoid what they don't want) is to appeal to a compelling interest of a parent.

As this illustration shows, however, there is often a fine line between negotiation and manipulation. As sinners, children will naturally attempt to use their powers of persuasion in dishonest and selfish ways. They will be tempted to give us a special smile before asking for a new toy, or tell us only what we want to hear when seeking permission to spend time with a questionable friend.

As parents, we need to ask God to give us discernment and wisdom to guard against being manipulated by our children. At the same time, we need to cooperate with God's sanctifying work in their lives, and ask Him to use us in helping them to develop and use their natural negotiation skills in godly ways.

Corlette and I first began to teach our children negotiation skills by teaching them a simple method of appealing decisions we made that affected them. As explained in more detail in Corlette's book *The Young Peacemaker,* this method involves two steps. First they make a respectful "I statement," and then they ask a question. For example, "I know you asked me to empty the garbage, Mommy. Daddy is leaving for work in a few minutes, and I would like to talk with him about my birthday party before he goes. May I please talk with him first and then empty the garbage?"

When they grew older, we had our children memorize Philippians 2:3-4. "Do nothing out of selfish ambition or vain conceit, but in humility consider others better than yourselves. Each of you should look not only to your own interests, but also to the interests of others." We then sought to use the conflicts of daily life as opportunities to teach them the key step in the negotiation process, namely, to understand and look out for the interests of others.

For example, when Jeff wanted Megan to share one of her toys with him, we encouraged him to offer her one of his toys in exchange. When they squabbled over which video to watch, we told them they could not watch any video unless both agreed on one, which gave each of them incentive to find one that the other would enjoy. And when one of them wanted help with his or her chores, we urged him or her to think of benefits to offer the other person to motivate cooperation.

As our children grow older, we should continue to help them develop the ability to understand others' interests. One way to do this is to involve them in the process of making certain substantive decisions that directly affect them. This can include deciding which toys we buy for them, which friends they spend time with, how long they can be away from home, what clothes they wear, and what the family does for fun on Saturday.

Instead of simply dictating to them on such issues, we can encourage them to discern the interests that other family members have in these decisions. For example, Daddy would rather spend money on sturdy toys that won't break in five minutes. Mommy wants them to have friends that model respectful behavior. Both parents want them to dress modestly. And the whole family can have fun if we go to the beach instead of going to a ball game only the boys will enjoy.

As we seek to involve our children in deciding these types of issues, we should teach them to respect our responsibility and authority to make the final decision. Whether they like that decision or not, they should comply with it. When our children grumble about our decisions, we usually withdraw the privilege of making appeals or participating in the decision-making process for a few days. Since they have a strong interest in retaining these privileges, they have learned that it is to their advantage to cheerfully accept our decisions, even when those decisions are not their preference.

As children grow older, we can teach them the full PAUSE negotiation process: Prepare. Affirm relationships. Understand interests. Search for creative solutions. Evaluate options reasonably and objectively (see chapter 7). As they develop these skills, the family can work together more smoothly to look out for each other's interests in a wide variety of substantive issues. At the same time, we will be preparing our children to be godly negotiators later in life, whether in their own families, churches, or careers.

AS YOU GROW

When you experience conflict with your children, you have an opportunity to point them to God, help them to grow, and strengthen your relationship with them. Here are some ways to make the most of these opportunities.

1. Glorify God, not sinful behavior. That is, instead of dwelling on what your child is doing wrong and how it is making your life difficult, focus your thoughts, prayers, and words on God: who He is, what He has done, and what He promises to do for those He loves.

2. Get the log out of your own eye. Recognize the idols that guide your parenting (comfort, convenience, control, how we look to others, etc.). Confess them to God and ask Him to free you from them. And if they have recently led you to sin against your children, confess the sin to them and ask for their forgiveness. Your example in confessing and renouncing your sin will teach your children far more effectively than a thousand mini-lectures.

3. Go and show your brother his fault, always ministering the gospel. When our children have been caught up in conflict or sin, it is natural for us to point out all the things they have done wrong. But if all we do is hit them over the head with the law, we will burden and discourage them. We must also bring the gospel to bear, reminding them that Jesus came to pay for their sin, to offer forgiveness, and to give them freedom from the idols that mess up their lives.

4. Go and be reconciled. When your children have deeply hurt you, it is easy to punish them by withholding forgiveness, even after they have confessed their wrongs. But that is not how God treats us. He is so willing to forgive us the moment we look to Him! Ask Him to help you imitate His unmerited love and forgiveness to your family, so that through you they will get a daily taste of God's amazing grace.

5. Use conflict to teach godly negotiation. Children are natural negotiators; they are often looking for a way to get what they want, or
   avoid something they do not want. Help your child use these negotiation skills in ways that please God—that is, by making respectful appeals and looking out for the interests of others.

DIGGING DEEPER

For further guidance on how to resolve conflict with children, see:

▮ *The Young Peacemaker*, by Corlette Sande
▮ *Age of Opportunity*, by Paul David Tripp
▮ *The New Dare to Discipline*, by Dr. James Dobson

10

Conflict Between Adult Family Members

"Happy families are all alike," Russian novelist Leo Tolstoy opined back in the 1800s, but "every unhappy family is unhappy in its own way." True enough, so far as it goes. But as the reach of almost all generalizations exceeds their grasp, this one has some holes. For unhappiness within families almost always has the same root problem: unresolved conflict.

The son clashes with dad; the daughter doesn't get along with mom. Or maybe it's son versus mom, daughter versus dad. The daughter and son fight with each other. The children stretch the patience of the parents during the teen years. Then when the daughter and son choose their life partners, they throw more personalities into the family stew—in-laws, children, aunts and uncles. More individuals are added to the family mix, all with their own personalities, their own interests, their own priorities. The bowl of tomato soup that was the nuclear family of father, mother, and kids can become, with the additional ingredients, a tureen of five-alarm chili.

Whatever the issues of conflict, the peacemaking principles given in Scripture give a family the best chance to resolve their difficulties in a way that benefits them and honors God.

Tolstoy didn't try these principles out on his fictional families, and we wouldn't have *Anna Karenina*, from which the opening quotation is taken, if he had. So let's see how they play out in the lives of another fictional family, the Crawfords.

George Crawford was a military man from the tips of his spit-shined shoes to the top of his crew-cut head. Even now, in retirement, the ex-Air Force colonel cut an imposing figure, especially when he stretched his 6'3" frame to its full height, as he usually did when hearing bad news.

"The bottom line, Dad," he was hearing on the phone, "is that Carla and I won't even be going through St. Louis. So we *can't* stop and see you and Mom."

"It's right on the way, Matt," George returned. "A straight shot. Indianapolis. St. Louis. The Colorado mountains. Freeway all the way. Couldn't be any more direct."

"We're going north, Dad."

"That's out of your way by a couple hundred miles!"

"That's what we want to do."

George paused. "What are you doing with the twins?"

"They're staying with the Terwilligers, a couple from church."

"Let's see if I've got this straight," George said briskly. "You and Carla are driving from Indianapolis to Colorado for a week in the mountains. And rather than drop your boys off with us, which is right on the way, and which would allow your mother to see them for a week, you're driving way the heck out of your way to get there and you're leaving Timmy and Tommy with somebody from your church?"

"That's what I just said."

"You care so little about your mother, who has been quite sick for quite a long time, in case you've forgotten, that you will deny her the pleasure of seeing her son for a day or two and her grandchildren for a week?"

"I didn't say *that*."

"That's what it amounts to."

"Look, Dad," Matt said. "That's what we decided to do."

"Sounds to me like you're avoiding us."

"We'll drop them off some other time."

"That's what you said at Easter."

"We were there at Christmas."

George paused. Then: "Pammy stayed three days when she and Dan went to New England in June. Left Esther and Carol here too."

Matt sighed. "What my sister does with herself and her kids is her business."

"She had enough concern for your mother to come see her and to let her have a week with those two darling little girls."

"She can do whatever she wants."

"It was even out of their way."

"Dad!"

"St. Louis is *not* on the way from the Twin Cities to New England."

"Will you quit it!"

George sighed. "You disappoint me, Matt."

"Come on, Dad. Not this."

"And not me so much, but your mother."

"Don't go there, Dad."

"Hear me out, Matt."

"I've heard you out for *26 years*, Dad," Matt said, his voice rising. "I'm tired of hearing you out."

"Some gratitude, that's all I can say."

Matt pulled himself together. "All I'm saying, Dad, is that I'm married and on my own now. I've got a wife and two kids, and we're making our own decisions." He took a deep breath. "And our decision for the trip to Colorado is to go up to I-80 and then across."

"That's final, then?"

Matt was getting riled again. "Yes, it's final. It was final 10 minutes ago when we started talking. And it's still final!"

"I see," George said. He paused. "I'm going to hang up now and attend to your mother."

"Dad!"

"What?"

"I don't want our conversation to end this way."

"As you said, Son, you made your plans," George said. "And the fact is, now that you're all grown up, your father and sick mother do not figure much in those plans."

"Dad!"

"Good-bye, Son." Matt heard the click but held the receiver to his ear a long time, a strange brew of guilt and exhilaration washing over him—guilt at disappointing his mother, exhilaration at standing up to his dad.

So ended the latest installment in what had become a series of tense conversations between Matt and his parents. Actually, it began way back in high school when Matt started coming of age, when he developed an independent streak that did not sit well with his mother, Neta, or his father either—that is, when the latter was around.

Oh, Dad called the shots, for sure. But he was out of town more than he was in it, away for extensive tours of duty. That left the disciplinary regimen to Neta, who was intensely loyal to her husband and no more lenient in meting out correction than he was. She didn't like her son's "pigheaded stubbornness," as she called it, any more than George did. And when Matt married Carla when they were both 19 rather than delaying the vows as George and Neta had encouraged, Neta felt a deep hurt while her husband went through the roof.

Carla took their disapproval personally. And when she and Matt had the twins, Timmy and Tommy, she resented her in-laws' requests—"constant demands," she called them—for time with the youngsters. She wanted to keep a respectful distance between her family and her in-laws, even a permanent "respectful distance." She urged Matt to stand up to his dad, and figured her life would be just fine, thank you very much, if she never even saw her in-laws again.

One in-law in her perpetual doghouse was Pammy, who called 10 minutes later. Pammy is not one for pleasantries. She launched right in with, "Dad called me. What's this about you avoiding them?"

"We're not avoiding them," Matt said. "We're just not going through St. Louis this time."

"You're punishing Mom. Did you know that?"

"No, we're not," Matt said. "That's ridiculous."

"What do you have against her, not visiting her and denying her access to your kids?"

"I don't have anything against her."

"That's what you're doing, you know. Denying Mom access to you, and denying her access to Timmy and Tommy. She loves them as much as she loved you and me."

"You, maybe." Matt could fight too.

"What do you mean by that?"

"Oh, you were always her favorite."

"That's crazy."

"Dad's favorite too."

There was silence.

Matt continued: "It was always 'Pammy this' and 'Pammy that.' Look how Pammy follows orders. Look how nice Pammy's friends are."

"You're even pettier than I thought."

"It wasn't Pammy who suffered when Dad decided to move us to Tampa during my junior year in high school."

"He was transferred, Matt."

"He didn't have to take it!"

"Oh, I get it now. Dad should put his military career on hold so as not to disrupt his son's promising high school football career, making him go to a big school where he couldn't be star quarterback anymore."

"He could have waited a year. That's all I'm saying."

"You still haven't forgiven them for having the guts to punish you for being so wild. You were uncontrollable back then and deserved everything you got from them."

"And you were a real angel too, huh, Pammy?"

"At least I didn't choose a selfish, insensitive spouse."

"What does Carla have to do with this?"

"She put you up to this, didn't she?"

"Huh?"

"Not going through St. Louis. It was her idea, right?"

"No. We decided we wanted to go a different way, that's all."

"I don't believe you."

"Well, it's true."

"Nice woman, Matt. Keeping her kids from seeing their grandma and grandpa."

"I am not going to listen to you put down Carla," Matt said. "Goodbye." And this time it was he who hung up.

▌ ▌ ▌

What a family! Year after year they labored with the same painful patterns. A father, ex-military, who lays down the law in the family. Who wants his kids—and everyone else—to respect his wisdom and defer to his advice. Who is intensely devoted to his ailing wife.

A mother who sacrificed for her husband throughout her life, enforcing in her husband's frequent absences the discipline he handed down from on high, following without complaint when he uprooted the family every couple years for a new position in a new town. Who is now in ill health—12 surgeries in 10 years. Who loves her grandchildren and is cheered immeasurably by their presence.

A son who rebelled early and often. Who has grown up emotionally and wants to be out from under his parents' thumb, yet also wants them to respect him as his own man. Who doesn't want them to push him around but longs to retain amicable connections with them. Who has a wife and kids whom he loves devotedly but a sister he still resents for being the parents' favorite when they were kids.

A daughter-in-law who urges her husband to stand up to his parents and live his own life. Who is protective of her kids. Who has had it up to *here* with in-laws of all shapes and sizes and wants nothing to do with them ever again.

And a daughter who is unflinchingly loyal to her parents. Who takes their side in family disputes. Who thinks her brother married a selfish, insensitive woman. Who loves to butt into others' business.

APPLYING THE FOUR G'S

The Crawfords' family dynamics are complex, but with God's grace they can be changed. Let's see how the use of the Four G's of conflict resolution could transform these strained relationships.

Glorify God

You didn't have to tell any of the Crawfords that they were sinners. Neta and the kids had frequently been reminded of it—George made sure of that—and George harbored no illusions about his own sinfulness before God. But they could certainly benefit from hearing—and inwardly embracing—the fact that they were *redeemed* sinners.

A key goal in any family conflict is to give testimony to the redeeming and life-changing power of Christ; to remember who we are in our own flesh first, and then who we are in Christ. Jesus' death and resurrection had changed the Crawfords' eternal itinerary, and His Spirit that dwelt within them was fully capable of guiding their steps through this life's stages as well. Each family member must truly understand and believe this good news, then proclaim it, both verbally and through their actions.

So the question each one of the Crawfords had to answer was this:

How can I give witness to what Christ has done and is doing in me? How can what I say and what I do, and how I interact with other family members, give glory to Christ?

This is key to resolving any family conflict. It radically changes family members' perspectives. It dramatically alters their priorities. Having an attitude of witness to Christ pries our eyes off ourselves and what we want and fixes them on God and His goals.

The Crawfords, each one of them, need to internalize this redeeming grace. They must keep this question, "How can I glorify God?" ever in their minds as they seek resolution to their family problems.

Get the Log Out of Your Own Eye

At the same time, the Crawfords must probe directly to the heart of the conflict. Picking around the edges not only delays progress in resolving a conflict, but also obscures the issue and frequently creates additional problems, even more potential conflicts.

At the heart of this conflict, as in so many, are desires that have been turned into demands and are controlling family members' thoughts and actions. Such desires are not necessarily *bad* things. When kept in proper perspective, they are in fact often good. But when elevated to unequivocal demands, they become idols, false gods family members pursue to the detriment of their relationship with God and amicable relationships with each other.

Each of the Crawfords had at least one:

- Neta's desire to see and enjoy her grandchildren frequently.
- George's desire for his children to be sensitive to Neta's health problems and treat her respectfully.
- George's desire to guide his children and for them to recognize the wisdom of his ideas.
- Matt and Carla's desire not to be controlled or manipulated.
- Matt and Carla's desire not to be inconvenienced by visitation.
- Matt's desire for love from and acceptance by his parents.
- Matt's desire for his parents to make up for perceived inequities in the way they treated him and his sister, Pammy, when they were young.
- Carla's desire for George and Neta to treat Matt with respect.
- Pammy's desire that George and Neta be deferred to in all family squabbles.

Again, none of these desires are sinful in and of themselves. Only when they began to consume the family members and rule their lives did they damage the family relationships.

The governing principle in solving conflicts with others is that *confession leads to forgiveness.* This same principle is at the heart of our relationship with God; it is equally crucial for family harmony.

For the Crawfords to make any movement toward peace in their family, they have to lay out their sins and request forgiveness. But who is to confess? George? Neta? Matt? Carla? Pammy? Each of them has elevated a desire to a demand and sinned against others. Ideally, each of them should confess.

So how does a family get started on the path to confession and forgiveness? We do not live in an ideal world. If even one family member sincerely confesses his or her sin, that will be a remarkable thing! And in some cases, that one confession might inspire one or two others to admit their contribution to the problem. Even if some family members fail to confess all of their sins, those who do will have at least started the family back in the direction of reconciliation.

As we saw in chapter 4, the confession process begins with one person making a prayerful examination of his or her contribution to the conflict. This examination will deal with three areas: words, actions, and attitudes and motivations.

Once one's wrongs are identified, family members could individually approach their heavenly Father and ask for forgiveness. Then they would seek out the offended parties for a face-to-face confession. Doing so in the physical presence of the others sends strong—and positive—signals. It shows respect for the other—that they feel so strongly about the matter that they will inconvenience themselves to the point that they show up in person to make things right.

Choosing the proper time and place is also crucial for success. The best place is one where the offended party will feel comfortable and relaxed, a place where the atmosphere encourages open and sincere dialogue. The timing should be open-ended. Neither should be detained by commitments before the talk, nor hurried by commitments scheduled afterward.

Unfortunately, logistics often make such face-to-face confession impractical. This is the case for the Crawfords. The parents live in St. Louis; one child in Indianapolis; another in Minneapolis. To begin resolving the dispute, they may have to talk by telephone. But even then, they can choose a time to call that they know would be convenient for the other, and they should certainly ask if they are calling at a good time, when no scheduled commitments could interfere with their conversation. They may even want to place a call to schedule the follow-up call of confession. This would have an effect similar to a face-to-face meeting—it says they're concerned enough to call once to schedule the confession, and then call again for the confession proper.

Family members should also plan their words. It is true, conversations are by their very nature unscripted endeavors; they are give-and-take oral communication, with both parties responding spontaneously to what the other says. But opening statements need not be. So the confessor in each case would be wise to think through exactly what he or she wants to open with and commit it to paper. (Review again the Seven A's of Confession in chapter 4 to make sure you cover all pertinent areas in your confession.)

In the Crawfords' case, some of these opening statements might look like this:

- From Matt to George: "I have dug in my heels against you and Mom on many occasions in recent years. I have allowed my sinful pride and desire for independence to dictate my actions toward you and Mom. My pride governed Carla's and my decision not to go through St. Louis on our way to Colorado. There was no reason for us to take an alternate route other than my selfish attitude. I was wrong to deprive the twins from sharing in your and Mom's love. I know this has hurt you two deeply. I also know that my prideful attitudes and sinful actions are displeasing to God. I'm very sorry for being so selfish and unloving toward you and Mom. If the offer is still open, we'd love to drop off the boys in St. Louis on our way to Colorado."

- From George to Matt: "Son, I could tell during our telephone conversation last week that I upset you with my words and attitudes. I was manipulative and unloving and unfair to both you and Carla. I know how angry I would get during my Air Force days when other officers would pull the same stunt on me, and I can only imagine the frustration and hurt you must feel when you get it from your own father. I have a great deal of sinful pride. I often think I'm right and everybody else is wrong. And I try to control people. You are a grown man, standing on your own two feet, and too often I've treated you like you were still living under my roof. Your decision on where to go on vacation and how to get there is your business, and I made it mine. It would make me very happy if you could find it in your heart to forgive my sinful actions and words, and even thoughts, toward you and Carla."

▌ From Carla to George: "You must be very frustrated and hurt that I have been so distant from you and Mom. I also know how much you love our two boys and enjoy being near them. It was wrong for me to withhold that pleasure from you. I'm sorry I've hurt you. I promise to try in the future to be more considerate of you and Mom. Will you please forgive me?"

▌ From Pammy to Matt and Carla: "I made harsh and untrue statements to Matt on the telephone last week. I said bad things about Carla too. I also have a bad habit of sticking my nose into affairs that are none of my business. With God's help, I promise to try to stop doing that. Will you forgive me?"

Again, it is highly unlikely that everyone would acknowledge his or her own sin this fully at the outset of the conversation. But if only one or two of them are able to humble themselves this way, it will start the conversation moving in the right direction.

As you read these statements, notice the absence of qualifiers, of *if's*, *but's*, *maybe's*, and *perhaps's*. Confession is not the place to justify your actions or minimize your guilt. It's not the time for Matt, for example, to say, "I shouldn't have withheld my family's affections from Mom, but you know, Dad, you make me so mad when you try to control me all the time." A "confession" like that would only fuel the fire. Be brutally honest about yourself in these confessions, and don't bring the other party's actions into it in a way that might seem to be taking the focus off of your own wrongs.

Go and Show Your Brother His Fault, Always Ministering the Gospel

Confession can open the door for relaxed communication. When you say, "I was wrong," others will often respond in kind, saying, "Well, it wasn't all your fault...."

But counter-confessions are often not as thorough as they need to be. Therefore, we need to know how to move from confessing to lovingly confronting family members who have not fully faced up to their contribution to a conflict.

This can be a daunting task; indeed, it is often painful, all the more so because we are dealing with family. In chapter 5, we looked at several basic principles for successful confrontation. Key elements include: overlooking minor offenses; picking an appropriate place and time for the talk; employing the five listening skills (waiting, attending, clarifying, reflecting, and agreeing); and building up and not tearing down with our words.

I want to emphasize again the importance of always ministering the gospel when confronting others. This approach doesn't discount the importance of the other's sin; it merely puts it in context. And that context is the marvelous news that although we have all drifted far from God in the same sinful heart condition, rescue is available through the good news of Jesus' death and resurrection.

By emphasizing how God's love can change another's behavior and attitude, we are believing the best about him or her and holding out hope through the promises of Jesus Christ. This hope is available; it is accessible; it can change hearts and minds. Indeed, God can use the family situation, however dire it may be, as an opportunity for all family members to grow in Christ.

This is the approach the Crawfords could take in resolving their squabbles. Whoever is willing to step out first could follow the suggestions in chapter 5 about how to phrase their concerns—using "I" statements and speaking kindly and gently. George could describe the pain he feels when Matt and Carla do not seem to show concern for his wife's health problems, and that they do not seem to respect his wisdom as much as he would like. Neta could explain how hurt she feels when she can't see her grandchildren as often as she would like. Matt could share how George's attempts to control his behavior make him feel. Carla's words would be about feeling pushed around and manipulated. Pammy's would deal with her desire to see her parents' wishes respected.

But each confronter could also add something like this: "Jesus died for your sins as well as mine. He paid for all of them on the cross. He has come into my heart and forgiven me of my selfish, prideful desires. With His help, I am determined to change my attitudes and behaviors toward you and everyone else in the family. And He can help you to do the same. You can receive this forgiveness just as I did when I confessed my sins against God and you. All you have to do is ask. I hope and pray that you will do that, because I dearly want to reconcile our differences and enjoy a closer friendship in the future."

These are powerful words, which God may use to soften others' hearts. When that happens, you can move toward reconciliation. But this is not always the case. Even when we confess our wrongs and confront others as gently and thoughtfully as possible, they may refuse to forgive us or face up to their wrongs. (In a case as intense as the Crawfords', it would be unusual for all of the family members to move toward reconciliation at the same pace; even if some confess and forgive quickly, others are likely to take months to work through their feelings.)

If unresolved issues leave a noticeable wall between you and another person, you may need to seek the involvement of a neutral third party who can serve as a mediator and help you to resolve your differences (Matthew 18:16). This may be a trusted relative or family friend, a leader in your church, a trained reconciler, or a professional counselor. Obviously, the person selected to mediate must be acceptable to all in the family (see Appendix C for suggestions on how to contact a trained reconciler in your church or community).

If other family members agree to mediation, God may work through that person to enable you to overcome offenses that have divided your family for years. If they refuse, God can still bless you, using their stubbornness to refine your character and help you to develop the Christ-like ability to love others even when they are not loving you (Luke 6:27-28; James 1:3-4; Romans 12:14-21).[1]

Go and Be Reconciled

Forgiveness can be especially difficult in family conflicts, primarily because expectations of each other are high and the sense of betrayal can be intense. And then there's family history. As much as we may want to forget the past, previous patterns of hurtful behavior are not deleted from our memory banks once a new confession is made. We may tell the person who hurt us that we forgive, but old hurts often linger in our minds and cloud subsequent interactions.

To remove these clouds from our relationships, we need to ask God to help us forgive as He has forgiven us. As we have seen in chapter 6, one way to do this is to commit ourselves to the four promises of forgiveness: I will not think about this incident; I will not bring up this incident again and use it against you; I will not talk to others about this incident; and I will not allow this incident to stand between us or hinder our personal relationship.

George Crawford, for example, could commit himself to not dwell on his son's insensitivity toward Neta. He would not put it in his ammunition cache for future deployment—a dirty, but all too common, tactic in any argument. He wouldn't indulge Pammy's desire for "dirt" on Matt and Carla. And he would not pull back from Matt and Carla, being distant on the phone.

Matt's promises would follow a similar course. He would dedicate himself to not dwelling on his dad's attempt to control his behavior. He wouldn't dig out of his memory bank past instances when George tried to control him and fire them back in his father's face. He wouldn't complain about his dad to any third party, not even his wife. And he would not allow any perceived slight to influence his next interaction with his dad.

Easier said than done, you say? Of course it is. Only God can offer forgiveness of this quality. Our forgiveness of others, while modeled after and inspired by God's forgiveness of us, is inferior to it. It lacks the quality, and duration, of God's unprecedented and absolute forgiveness, and may always be tainted with a tendency to dwell on the sin and hold it against the confessor.

Sometimes, however, the roadblocks to forgiveness are of our own making. These we can do something about. Occasionally the fault is with the confessor. Sins may be confessed superficially, casually, without the honest self-examination needed to get to the root of one's sin. In these cases the confessor should be urged to return to the Seven A's of Confession.

In other cases we cling to the notion that we want some kind of payment from the confessor. We want him or her to earn the forgiveness or to promise never, ever to commit that sin again. This we cannot do. God forgives us unconditionally and completely. So must we, even if the confessor may commit the same sin shortly after confessing to it. Our forgiveness of others can be no more conditional than God's forgiveness of us.

Especially effective in countering persistent negative thoughts—all too common in family relationships with long histories behind them—is the replacement principle. To employ this principle the person having trouble forgiving would replace the negative thought with a positive one (see pages 89-90 [in chapter 6]).

For example, when Matt Crawford starts dwelling on all the ways his dad has tried to control his behavior in his adult life, he would consciously choose to dwell on one or more of George's positive attributes —his Christian faith, his transmission of that faith to his family, his provision for the family all these years, his undying love for his wife. When Neta can't get her mind off how selfish she thinks Matt and Carla are with their kids, she should replace that with positive thoughts about Matt—his desire to provide for his family, his independence and trustworthiness at his occupation; and about Carla—her loving attitude toward Matt and her children. When Carla starts thinking about her in-laws, instead of firming her lips and slamming dishes into the dishwasher, she should think of George and Neta's love for her children, of Pammy's love for George and Neta. And if they find little to praise in one another, they can all fix their thoughts on God, giving thanks for all He has done in their lives in spite of their sins.

Both sides in the Crawford dispute could also make concrete efforts to be more amenable to the other side. George and Neta could avoid pushing for more visitation and instead look for ways to make visits easier and more convenient for their kids. Matt and Carla could consciously look for ways to accommodate his parents' requests as much as possible.

With a spirit not of competition but of cooperation, family members could then be freed up to seek practical solutions to the visitation problem. An effective way to go about this would be to negotiate using the PAUSE principle outlined in chapter 7.

As you recall, one of the chief steps in this principle is understanding interests (the U in PAUSE). Drawing on past conversations and experience with one another, the Crawfords could prayerfully identify the desires, fears, and concerns that need to be addressed to arrive at a mutually satisfactory solution. George's interests lie in serving his wife and being respected by his kids for his wisdom; Neta's lie in enjoying the love of her grandchildren; Matt's in being his own man;

Carla's in her family not being pushed around; and Pammy's in doing all she can so that her parents are happy and treated with respect.

Once the interests of others are uncovered, the family members could consider those interests as well as their own in seeking a creative solution to the visitation problem. Matt might ponder what would serve George and Neta's interests; George could consider what would serve Matt and Carla's. This strips the discussion of its competitive potential, turning it from a who-will-win matter to a how-can-we-solve-this endeavor. Everybody in the family could be pushing the same agenda—an amicable agreement that serves everybody's interests.

The S in PAUSE comes next—searching for solutions. When the Crawfords sit down to brainstorm, they could work together to identify creative ways to serve one another. By combining their efforts instead of working against one another, they stand a better chance of discovering ways to rebuild relationships and find ways to truly enjoy each other.

A variety of creative solutions could be tossed on the table. How about you coming over to Indianapolis occasionally? Matt asks. Yes, George responds, that would work. And thinking of Carla's role in the family, or her desire not to be saddled with in-laws for a week in her house, George recalls a friend of theirs in a small town near Indianapolis. He and Neta could visit them and drop by for a day or two. They could also meet in the middle, Matt suggests. George offers to pick up the motel bill to further that suggestion. Pammy says they could plan annual family reunions, a week spent at some scenic spot equidistant to all three families. A camp or condo somewhere. The three families would stay in separate cabins/rooms. Everybody kind of likes that idea.

At any rate, you get the idea. No suggestion is out of bounds in such a discussion. No question is stupid. Everybody gives a little, gains a little.

When the options are all placed on the table, the family as a whole evaluates them reasonably and objectively (the E in PAUSE). The Crawfords ask each other what problems each of the suggestions would create and whether these problems could be easily solved—whether, in short, the suggestions could work.

All agree that a family reunion at a "neutral" site would be workable.

Pammy volunteers to check out dates and prices for various camps and retreats in Midwestern states. She promises to report back to the family upon completion of her research, and all agree to try to schedule their lives to accommodate the dates.

The fact that the family openly discussed the problem, confessed their hurtful attitudes and actions, and forgave each other made everyone a little more sensitive to the interests of other family members. It got all of them outside their own little worlds, with their own issues and positions, and put them in a frame of mind to think of others' interests. Matt and Carla were more sensitive about sharing their lives and their children with George and Neta, and ended up going either through or to St. Louis far more often. George and Neta were more conscious of their son and daughter-in-law's need to live their own lives, and backed off from their demanding posture. Pammy began to appreciate her brother's perspective more as well.

God can heal family relationships no matter how divisive they are, and in time He healed the Crawfords' as well. George and Matt came closer together than they had ever been, resolving deep-seated issues both had more or less given up on. Carla began to see her in-laws' side of things when they made a special effort to befriend her and include her wishes in each solution. George and Neta came closer together, as George began to appreciate the stress his job and his many moves had put on his wife all those years. This had a positive effect even on Neta's health. And Pammy came to appreciate Carla, and vice versa. The fact that all were praying for one another was crucial in both reaching practical solutions for their problems and changing their hearts toward others in the family.

Family peace did not come easily or instantly to the Crawfords, but by God's grace, it did come over a period of several months. And when tensions developed subsequently, they had a foundation of good will on which to work, as they applied the same principles to confess and forgive, to talk and to listen, and to find solutions they could all enjoy.

WHAT IF IT'S WORSE THAN THIS?

As difficult as the Crawfords' situation was, other family conflicts I have been involved in have been much more complex. Some families are challenged by numbers alone. Four brothers and sisters find four wives and husbands. Each couple then has three or more children, who are also cousins and grandchildren, nephews and nieces. There are over two hundred different relationships within their circle alone. And each relationship provides the opportunity for misunderstanding, competition, and conflict.

Blended families, coming together after divorce shattered their original homes, must contend with an additional array of pressures: visitation and custody struggles, child support, children who play their parents and stepparents against one another, resentful and competitive siblings, and, all too often, a cloud of offenses that were never resolved in the divorce process, haunting the families for life.

Other families are thrown into intense turmoil by alcohol and drugs, mental problems, and adultery. The resulting compulsiveness, irrationality, and intense sense of betrayal can rob them of all trust as well as the ability to communicate reasonably and constructively.

And all too many families even in the church are crippled by a history of physical or sexual abuse that has never been acknowledged and confessed. There is an "elephant in the living room" that everyone has to step around but no one will talk about. Even if some family members want to maintain a relationship, denial of the problem by others prevents them from tearing down the walls and rebuilding trust. So their contacts are guarded, strained, and exhausting.

I have seen God bring about amazing reconciliation in these seemingly impossible situations. Sometimes He works through one or two family members who humbly, patiently, and persistently apply the peacemaking principles we have discussed in this book. More often, He brings a church leader or outside reconciler into the situation who has the gifting, objectivity, training, and experience needed to guide the family through the long process of repentance and restoration. (Even when there seems to be genuine repentance, in some situations, such as those involving sexual abuse, there will still be a need to maintain precautions against similar offenses.)

But many cases like these will never see a complete resolution in this life. No matter how hard some family members try to be reconciled, others harden their hearts and turn their backs on their own family.

If you are in a family that has yet to be reconciled, you need to recognize both your responsibilities and your limits. As God gives opportunity, you can seek to practice what you have learned in this book, not just once but perhaps again and again. And even if others refuse to talk with you, you can still pray for them and look for ways to bless and minister to them. As Paul taught the persecuted Romans, "'If your enemy is hungry, feed him; if he is thirsty, give him something to drink. In doing this, you will heap burning coals on his head.' Do not be overcome by evil, but overcome evil with good" (Romans 12:20-21).

But there are limits to what you can and should do. You can gently reach out, but only God can bring others to repentance (2 Timothy 2:24-26). Therefore, if a family member persists in hardening his or her heart, you may have to live with a stunted or guarded relationship, or you may have to settle for no relationship at all—at least for now. You never know what God might do tomorrow. You can continue to pray and wait patiently for the possibility that God will open up a new avenue of communication next month, or next year.

No matter what happens, you and your family are in God's loving hands. That alone is sufficient for peace and hope.

AS YOU GROW

No matter how old we are, we never lose our ability to fight with our parents or siblings. Therefore, we need to keep our peacemaking skills polished and ready for use at every stage of life. When we encounter conflict with those we love (or are angry with at the moment), it is always wise to return to the Four G's of conflict resolution:

1. Glorify God. Even though your family may be making life miserable for you, keep your focus on God and bring Him glory by constantly asking yourself, "How can I give witness to what Christ has done for me? How can what I say and what I do, and how I interact with other family members, bring praise to God and display the wonders of His grace?"

2. Get the log out of your own eye. When you fight with your mother or brother, you may be tempted to focus on what they have done wrong. They may then follow your example, point out your sins, and the downward spiral continues. Break this cycle by obeying Jesus' command to take the log out of your eye before focusing on the speck in others' eyes. By using the Seven A's of Confession (see chapter 4), you will not only deal with your sins thoroughly but also set an example that others may be inspired to follow.

3. Go and show your brother his fault, always ministering the gospel. If a family member is blind to his sin or fails to confess it adequately, and if it is too serious to overlook, the most loving thing you can do is graciously confront him so he can see where he needs to change. Be specific, be clear, listen carefully, and most of all, give hope by making the gospel central to your conversation.

4. Go and be reconciled. Families are for life. Conflict may hurt us and drive us apart, but God is always there to heal the wounds and restore our relationships. Ask Him to take away the hurt, anger, and bitterness, and to empower you to make the four promises of forgiveness. As you make and keep these God-imitating promises,

the hurtful memories will diminish, the pain will subside, and your family can once again demonstrate a love and unity that brings honor to God.

5. PAUSE. Family conflicts always provide opportunities to look out for others' interests as well as your own. Use these times to practice the five steps of the PAUSE principle of negotiating, which can not only resolve the immediate conflict but also deepen your appreciation for one another: prepare, affirm relationships, understand interests, search for creative solutions, and evaluate options.

Part 4

GETTING HELP

11

Getting Help for a Troubled Marriage

When Jack and Kathy tied the knot 10 years ago, they tied it with square knot upon square knot of heartfelt promises of never-ending fidelity. They both wanted their union to last, and they married with the most serious intent to make it do just that.

But there were problems from day one. Their biological clocks were different—he a morning person, she an evening person—as were their recreational tastes and emotional demeanors. Early on they were able to toss these differences aside—"Every marriage has its problems," they told each other—and carried on in more or less marital happiness.

But they did argue—about matters great and small. They disagreed about which car to buy and about every piece of furniture they purchased; they argued about diets and personal habits and tastes in music and movies and everything else, it seemed—no part of their lives together was immune from harangue. Early in their marriage they didn't see these arguments as any big deal, and their desire to be happy would move Kathy to make peace one time and Jack another time. But soon one or the other would feel he or she was giving in too often and would subsequently stand his or her ground.

And in time one or the other would become emotionally detached. Rather than subjecting himself to what he termed Kathy's "constant nagging," Jack took up golf—and with a passion. So great was his love for this sport—or for being away from his wife—that Kathy threatened to leave him. "Since I'm a golf widow already," she said, "I might as well make it official and go live with my sister." That got Jack's attention, and he shaped up for a while. Another time it was Jack who threatened departure. He couldn't take Kathy's penchant to analyze and interpret his every word, his every action—the "constant nagging" that led him to take up golf in the first place. In response Kathy was more agreeable for a few months.

Suffering from each succeeding fight and "reconciliation," however, were affection, intimacy, and even interest in each other. By their tenth anniversary they were hardly ever expressing their love for each other, either physically or verbally. They talked some, over dinner and in front of the television, but it was cursory and very safe conversation, a far cry from the mutual baring of the soul they had engaged in when first married.

Then at Jack's company's Christmas party, something happened. Kathy noticed that Jack and a coworker, Wanda, seemed a little too chummy. Kathy knew Wanda too—she was a single woman who attended their church. But there was something about how her husband was acting around Wanda that bothered Kathy—he was the same funny, congenial, happy man she had been drawn to when they first courted. She hadn't seen that Jack for about five years.

She asked Jack about Wanda, and Jack told her he found Wanda understanding and kind. "She's fun to be around," he said. They hadn't taken their flirtatious repartee to the physical level, Jack said, and he vowed not to let that happen.

But to Kathy it was a wake-up call. She saw her union with Jack in serious jeopardy and wondered what she should do.

▮ ▮ ▮

The facts about divorce in our society are not encouraging. Between 45 and 50 percent of U.S. marriages end in divorce, experts say. Indeed, one of every six adult Americans is expected to have two or more divorces during their life. We as a society have come to view marriage as similar to occupations—expendable when we feel the need for a change. Even within the Christian fold, divorce has become so common that many pastors have opted for this once unthinkable way to resolve marriage problems within the church.

Many of these divorces could be prevented if marriage partners knew where to look for problem areas in their marriages and what to do about them once discovered. This chapter will discuss "reactive steps" a couple can take when they find themselves in a troubled marriage but have failed to lay the groundwork for help.

WHEN TO GET HELP

Marriage, like life, often has its ebbs and flows, its ups and downs. It is only natural that partners in a long-term relationship are going to feel closer to each other at some times than at others. However, when the tide goes out but does not quickly come back in, or when the relationship goes south and stays there for an uncomfortably long period, you need to take note. Here are some warning signs you should look for:

▮ You sense a steady decline in respect, affection, or love for your spouse.

▮ Your conversations are growing increasingly superficial.

▮ You feel less and less desire to be with your spouse and a growing desire to be doing things away from your spouse.

▮ You talk repeatedly about the same issues without making noticeable progress in resolving them.

▮ You argue frequently or with intense anger.

▮ You go through lengthy periods of unforgiveness.

▮ You or your spouse seem to be attracted to another person.

One or more of these signs may mean your marriage is in trouble. The question then becomes: What do I do about it?

In most cases, the first thing to do is to talk with your spouse. Using the principles discussed in the first seven chapters of this book, carefully plan how to share your concerns. Avoid the temptation to blame or attack. Instead, use confession and the gospel to stimulate hope that things can get better. Be specific about your concerns and the consequences you may both face if you do not work together to improve your relationship. And then pray that the Holy Spirit will move your spouse to fight for your marriage too.

SEEKING COUNSEL

If personal conversations with your spouse are not fruitful, the next step may be to seek advice on what more you can do to individually to improve your marriage. We all have blind spots and set habits that are difficult to see and change. It may be that a neutral counselor can help you see your contributions to the problem more clearly and find ways to change and communicate more effectively with your spouse.

By striving first to change yourself, you may trigger a corresponding reaction in your spouse. This may enable you to improve your marriage even if both of you do not enter a counselor's office for a joint session. And if you eventually decide that both of you need outside help, any progress you make individually can help to show your sincerity in wanting to change, which may help to motivate your spouse to seek counseling with you.

It is essential that you choose a counselor who is biblically sound and is willing to say difficult but necessary things to you. Most of us have a natural tendency to seek counsel from people who we know will agree with us. Avoid these yes-men and yes-women. Also, be careful not to talk with others simply to criticize your spouse or to gain sympathy. This preliminary counsel is for you—you are seeking advice on how you, acting alone, can improve your marriage. Take the counsel seriously, and seek God's help to work as hard as you can to make whatever changes you can in yourself.

If your personal changes are not able to reverse the downward trend in your marriage, the next step is to persuade your spouse to join you in seeking advice on how to nurture your marriage. Do not be surprised if he or she is reluctant to seek counseling with you. There are several common reasons why one spouse is unwilling to seek counseling.

- He or she simply does not believe that there are serious problems, or if there are, they are all the other person's fault.
- Pride, making it difficult to admit he or she is wrong.
- Fearing what others may think if they learn you are having marital problems.
- Hopelessness, thinking it is a waste of time, because nothing is likely to change.
- Fearing that his or her own sins will be exposed.
- He or she just doesn't want to change or give up another relationship.

▌ Not knowing who to go to.

▌ Lack of money to pay for the counseling.

Knowing why your spouse may not want to join you in counseling is one thing. Persuading him or her to do it is quite another. For this endeavor, you may want to employ the PAUSE principles—the five negotiating principles we outlined in chapter 7.

Kathy, the partner wishing the counseling in our opening illustration, used these principles to broach the topic with her husband, Jack. She prepared (the P in PAUSE) by applying the Four G's to her own situation, confessing her own sins to God and trusting in Him to work in Jack's heart as well. She also affirmed her relationship with her husband (the A in PAUSE), much like Alice did in our illustration in chapter 7.

Crucial to her negotiation with Jack was the U, understanding her husband's interests. In order to be successful, her case for counseling would have to appeal to his interests. Jack treasured peace and quiet; he didn't like living in a house filled with strife and contention, or where argument was on the emotional menu night after night. So Kathy pointed out that counseling could help them to reduce the tension and friction that had marred their marriage over the years. It could also bring them closer together physically, could put the affection that enlivened the early years back into their relationship. She figured this would appeal to Jack.

She also knew Jack might be worried about what others would think if they knew their marriage was in trouble. Therefore, she emphasized the confidentiality of the counseling process. "We know that our pastor is counseling people all the time, and yet we've never heard one name or detail mentioned anywhere at church," she said. "And if he refers us to a Christian counselor outside the church, they are extremely careful in guarding confidentiality."

Then she contrasted for him the simple act of obtaining confidential counsel with the public scandal that would accompany a divorce. "Nobody has to know we're seeing a counselor, Jack," she said. "But if things don't get better and we end up in a divorce, *everybody* will know that."

Kathy had also done her homework. She had talked to other couples in their church, couples who had battled through difficult marital times and had emerged whole through the benefit of good Christian counseling. "Cynthia Rosburg shared with me that she and Pat went through counseling a few years ago, and Cynthia said it saved their marriage," Kathy said. This impressed Jack on two levels. First, he respected Pat Rosburg highly (which is one reason Kathy chose him as an illustration), which diminished Jack's embarrassment argument. Second, he didn't even know they had undergone counseling, which underlined Kathy's earlier point about confidentiality.

Then Kathy appealed to Jack's love of their children, who were still young and pretty much in the dark about their parents' troubles. She had done her research on this as well. She pointed out that respected studies have shown that children whose parents divorce are likely to suffer many negative side effects. They often blame themselves for the divorce, which creates debilitating guilt. They are inevitably hurt financially as the family takes on the cost of maintaining two households. They are more likely to have behavioral problems, to have difficulties at school, and to experience alcohol and drug abuse. Finally, their own marriages are more likely to end in divorce some day.

As Jack pondered these possibilities, counseling seemed more and more reasonable. The combined force of Kathy's arguments convinced Jack to join her in counseling. Kathy took it upon herself to research local counselors; they agreed on one; and the two began marriage counseling shortly after their discussion.

Other spouses will need more persuasion before they agree. For these it may be wise to ask a mature friend, someone your spouse trusts and respects, to meet with him or her and lay out the case for marital counseling.

If all else fails, you may need to ask your pastor or another godly advisor to initiate a conversation with you and your spouse. This is exactly what Corlette did with me during the first year of our marriage. A few months after we married, I became totally absorbed in building a garage. (A good thing had become a consuming idol.) I was neglecting our relationship and hurting my wife. Even though she repeatedly appealed to me to talk with our pastor, I put it off. Finally, in desperation, she invited our pastor into our home one afternoon. When I walked through the door after work and saw him sitting in the living room, I stopped dead in my tracks. I knew in an instant why he was there, and his mere presence convicted me of my sin. Even though I was somewhat angry to be caught off guard, I realized that it was really my fault. Corlette was completely justified in her actions and had shown far more concern about our relationship than I had. It did not take long for me to agree to some much-needed changes in my priorities. It was an embarrassing experience, but it changed the course of our marriage. And I know Corlette will do it again if I ever refuse to deal with important issues in our relationship!

CHOOSING THE RIGHT COUNSELOR

If you and your spouse are dealing with relatively minor problems, you will often be able to find all the help you need in a godly friend, relative, or couple. Since these people know you better than others do, they will often have deeper insights into your problem and be able to help you identify needed changes fairly quickly.

But sometimes it will not be appropriate to turn to family and friends. If you are dealing with complex or highly personal issues, it is generally wise to turn to people who can be more objective, have received training, and will not hold embarrassing revelations against you in the future.

When you need this kind of help with your marriage, you should usually look first to your own church. Ideally, your pastor or another godly leader or lay counselor should be able to help you bring God's Word to bear on your marital problems (Romans 15:14; Hebrews 13:17). In addition, the church should be able to support and encourage you and your spouse as you seek to grow and provide accountability as you work to overcome hard-to-break habits.

Sometimes, however, your church simply will not be able to meet your needs. Some pastors lack the gifting or training, or even the time, to deal with complex issues. In that case, you may need to look for a qualified Christian counselor in your community.

I cannot emphasize too strongly the need to seek counseling only from people who will offer you truly biblical advice. People who neither believe in Christ nor respect His Word may provide well-intended and occasionally helpful advice. But they are simply unable to fully comprehend God's design for marriage, the nature of sin, and what it takes to bring about true repentance and reconciliation (see 1 Corinthians 2:10-16). Therefore, their counsel will be unreliable. One moment they may offer a perfectly appropriate suggestion, but the next they may be leading you down a path that is completely contrary to God's Word.

Sadly, the same may be said about many sincere Christian counselors. Either because of deficient training, poor theology, a lack of genuine wisdom and experience, or misplaced sympathy, they mix biblical principles and solutions with those of the world. Much of what they say may be consistent with the Bible, but at crucial points, they turn aside and rely on their own opinions or secular psychology. Despite their good intentions, such counselors can lead you into spiritual disaster as easily as a person who denies Christ.

So how do you find a reliable Christian counselor? Start your search by asking your pastor or another leader in your church to recommend someone they have found to be biblically sound. Discerning friends or other pastors might be able to help you confirm a reference. As you narrow your search, you can ask potential counselors for information on their education, theology, and counseling methodology. Among other things, you should find out what their views are on the sufficiency of Scripture, the nature and role of sin in a marriage, how people change, and if and when they would recommend divorce. If their views in any of these areas fail to align with the clear teaching of the Bible, you should keep looking for a counselor who proves to be more biblically sound.

KEYS TO COUNSELING SUCCESS

Some couples spend years in counseling with few signs of progress. Others seem to resolve significant issues in just few weeks or months. If you want to get the most benefit out of marriage counseling as quickly as possible, there are five things you can do in addition to finding a solid biblical counselor.

First, focus on your responsibilities (Matthew 7:3-5). Many people come into counseling thinking their spouse is the one who most needs to change. The turning point in counseling occurs when one or both spouses begin to sincerely pray, "God, please improve my marriage, *starting with me.*" Although you can be an *influence* on your spouse, you are the only person in your marriage whom you can actually *change.* Therefore, the less you dwell on your spouse's deficiencies, and the more you seek to work with God as He changes you, the more quickly you will see progress in improving your marital relationship.

Second, go to the heart of your problems (James 4:1-3). As discussed in chapter 2, our tendency is to focus on surface behavior. To see lasting change in your marriage, you need to ask God, and sometimes a counselor, for help in identifying and forsaking the idols (desires-turned-into-demands) that are controlling your heart and undermining your marriage. Behavior patterns will change on a consistent basis only when the thoughts, attitudes, and desires that give rise to our words and actions have been fundamentally changed (Ephesians 4:24-26).

Third, remember the gospel (Romans 1:16). Jesus Christ came to deliver us from our sins. He has both the desire and the power to enable you and your spouse to put off your old ways, to develop radically new ways of thinking and behaving toward each other, and to give you a love for each other that surpasses anything you can imagine (Ephesians 3:20).

Fourth, ask for prayer support and accountability from within your church (James 5:16). Marriage counseling is a form of spiritual warfare—you are fighting against idols and worldly influences that threaten to destroy your marriage (Ephesians 6:10-18). Therefore, it is wise to seek out godly, discreet people who will respect your confidences and support you regularly in prayer and loving encouragement.

Finally, persevere. Most marriages get into trouble as a result of attitudes and habits that have developed over a long period of time, some of which preceded your wedding day. Since these problems took a long time to develop, they usually take a good deal of time and effort to resolve. Therefore, make a commitment to keep working as long as it takes to overcome problems that threaten your marriage, even if that means an extended season of counseling.

I have counseled many people who felt like their marriage had died and there was no point in going on. In response, I always remind them that we serve a God who resurrected His dead Son from the grave, and who promises to make that same resurrection power available to those who trust Him (Ephesians 1:18-20). Although many cases have still ended in divorce, I have personally witnessed God giving new life to countless marriages that seemed utterly beyond repair. So even if your marriage seems beyond repair, put your hope in God, depend on His grace, make every reasonable effort to reconcile, and trust God to work things out according to His plan.

A LAST RESORT

No matter how gently or persuasively you appeal to your spouse, he or she may not only refuse to seek or continue with counseling, but even decide to leave your marriage altogether. If this happens, it may be that your only remaining resort is to ask your church to exercise formal church discipline. This process is laid out by Jesus Himself in Matthew 18:15-17. He teaches that if informal, personal efforts to deal with sin do not succeed, we should "tell it to the church" (v. 17). This means that you should go to your church leaders and ask them to confront your spouse and exercise their ecclesiastical authority to promote repentance and reconciliation.

Sadly, many churches stopped obeying Jesus' commands in Matthew 18 decades ago. Even when marriages are falling apart before their very eyes, the leaders simply wring their hands and say they will pray—but do nothing more. When church leaders do have the courage to intervene lovingly and firmly in failing marriages, the mere threat of church discipline is sometimes all it takes to persuade a wayward spouse to turn around.[1] In other cases, however, an unrepentant spouse may simply harden his heart, leave the church, and proceed with a divorce. But even then, God sometimes continues to work through church leaders and fellow members who will not give up. This is what happened with Terri and Dave.

After many years of an unfulfilling marriage, Terri became involved with a coworker at the hospital. As she became increasingly interested in Scott, Terri started to pull away not only from her husband, Dave, but also from Christian friends who she knew would encourage her to stay in her marriage. Eventually, she left her husband and children, moved in with Scott, and filed for divorce. Her pastor tried repeatedly to talk with Terri, but she constantly avoided him. Finally, in a letter, he lovingly pleaded with her to remain faithful to her vows, and he offered for the church to provide or pay for whatever counseling it would take to help Terri and Dave resolve their differences and experience a fulfilling marriage.

Terri refused his offer and sent him a letter saying she was resigning from the church. Her pastor sent a final letter warning Terri of the spiritual consequences of breaking her vows and then he went to the congregation. In a meeting open only to church members, he explained that Terri had left her family and filed for divorce (which was a matter of public record). He then appealed to them to pray for her and, in the spirit of Matthew 18:12-14, to seek opportunities to lovingly appeal to her to return to her family. He also coached them on what to say if they saw her around town. Instead of treating her with contempt, or acting like nothing was wrong, he urged them to say something like this:

> Terri, it is so good to see you. I have missed seeing you at church. I know there have been difficulties in your marriage and you've filed for divorce. But it's not too late. If you honor your vows and accept the help the church will give you for counseling, your marriage can be restored. We love you and we want what is best for you. Please don't turn your back on God and your family.

Some church members deliberately contacted Terri to appeal to her, while others simply waited for God to providentially arrange encounters with her at the grocery store, in the mall, or on the sidewalk downtown. As a result, she heard this same basic appeal over and over.

More importantly, the Holy Spirit used her friends' words to convict Terri of her sin. At the same time, she could no longer ignore the effect her actions were having on her two young children, who were deeply frightened and hurt by the impending divorce. Moreover, Dave had been working diligently with their pastor to see how he had contributed to the breakdown of their marriage and needed to change. As he and Terri exchanged the children from week to week, Dave asked God to help him show Terri that he truly wanted to be a different man.

After four months of separation, numerous encounters with her family, and repeated appeals from her friends, Terri caved in. She finally saw that she was headed down a path that would inevitably lead to grief and misery for countless people. One day she walked unannounced into her pastor's office. "Is it too late?" she asked apprehensively. "Is there really a way to bring our family back together again?" With his enthusiastic assurances, Terri began a process of repentance and reconciliation.

After months of intense and sometimes difficult counseling, she and Dave worked out the many problems that had crippled their marriage, and they began to learn a new way of loving and relating to each other. It was not easy, but it was definitely worth the effort. When the day came for them to renew their vows, there were far more tears in the church than there had been on the day they married. To acknowledge the church's key role in restoring her marriage, Terri asked their pastor to read Jesus' words from Luke 15:4-6 as part of the ceremony:

> Suppose one of you has a hundred sheep and loses one of them. Does he not leave the ninety-nine in the open country and go after the lost sheep until he finds it? And when he finds it, he joyfully puts it on his shoulders and goes home. Then he calls his friends and neighbors together and says, "Rejoice with me; I have found my lost sheep."

Of course many lost sheep will not respond as Terri did. They will harden their hearts, and no matter how hard we try, they will not turn back. But God does not hold you responsible for what others do, only for what you do (Romans 12:18). Look to Jesus, follow what He commands, and leave the results to Him. No matter what happens, you will be able to move on in life with a clear conscience and a peace that transcends understanding.

AS YOU GROW

If you believe your marriage may be in danger, now is the time to take action. The longer you wait, the more likely it is that further damage will occur. There are several practical steps to take to save a troubled marriage.

1. Analyze the problem. Make a list of warning signs, noting whether they are isolated incidents or part of an ongoing pattern.

2. Talk with your spouse. Using the principles discussed in the first seven chapters of this book, carefully plan how to present your concerns to your spouse.

3. Seek counsel. If the two of you cannot resolve your differences alone, seek help from a godly counselor. Try to anticipate why your spouse may be hesitant to seek help, and ask God to help you think of persuasive ways to overcome these obstacles.

4. Pray and persevere. As you approach each counseling session, repeat the prayer, "God, please improve my marriage, beginning with me." Remember who you are in Christ—forgiven and redeemed!—and trust His promise that He is committed to changing you and your spouse. You may not see dramatic changes at first; many marital problems take years to develop, so they may also take weeks or months to resolve.

5. Finally, look to your church for counsel, support, and, if necessary, redemptive church discipline. Remember that the battle is worth it, and bring honor to God by persevering in your efforts to save the marriage that He brought you into.

DIGGING DEEPER

For more information on dealing with a spouse who refuses to be reconciled, see:

- *The Peacemaker: A Biblical Guide to Resolving Personal Conflict* (pages 168-180)
- *Love Must Be Tough,* by Dr. James Dobson
- *Hope for the Separated,* by Gary Chapman

12

Insurance Policies for a Healthy Marriage

Chuck and Brenda looked right together. Whether it was sitting in a pew singing from a shared hymnal at church on Sunday morning or rolling their cart up and down the grocery store aisles, playfully debating which supplies to buy for an upcoming party during the week, they were what disinterested observers would call "made for each other."

And it showed. The physical compatibility was certainly there— why, you hardly ever saw them *not* holding hands. They shared many of the same interests and books. Ditto for recreational compatibility— both loved sports, and in fact, the same sports. As for their spiritual lives, when Chuck took a promising entry level position in a growing Sun Belt-city firm shortly after they married, the couple eagerly joined a rapidly growing church, where they were one happy couple among what appeared to be many.

When they had children a few years into their marriage, however, clouds started to dim this sunny prospect. The kids were beautiful—bright, healthy, adorable—and Brenda threw herself totally into their lives. Whether it was T-ball or swimming, clarinet lessons or kiddie choir, she enrolled her youngsters in all of them, and was there every moment overseeing their every move—glorying in their little victories, suffering in their little defeats. And as sometimes happens, she started living her life vicariously through them.

While Jason and Mindy may have been receiving all the love their mother could give them, Chuck meanwhile was feeling ignored. Oh, he loved the kids too, and he showed it, but his love was no match for Brenda's—she made certain of that—so he fled to the comfortable refuge of his work. Ten- or twelve-hour days at the office became the rule, not the exception, and because the intimacy he had once shared with Brenda was diminishing by the month, he didn't feel guilty about it one little bit.

He also sought out new recreational activities to take his mind off his problems at home. Good at most sports but just a passable tennis player, he signed up for lessons at a club, and there his extracurricular sports became extramarital as well. Dinah, a divorcée who taught tennis for a living, liked what she saw in Chuck and gave him extra tutelage with his strokes. One thing led to another, and soon the two were cutting short their lessons on the court only to take them up again in Dinah's apartment.

A couple months of this, and one day Chuck walked into the kitchen with divorce papers in hand. He was in love, he told Brenda, with somebody who "cares about me a whole lot more than you do," and he wanted out of this "loveless" marriage.

Brenda didn't want out—at least not at first. She appealed to their church for help, but her pastor refused to talk with Chuck. Early in his pastoral career, he had confronted an adulterous husband, and the backlash made him vow he would never do it again. Besides, he reasoned, it's probably better for the kids not to be in a home where there is no love and lots of fighting.

So Brenda wrote off the marriage, but she would not budge on the kids. She fought the custody battle with a vengeance, and with the wounds still fresh and the blood still flowing, the divorce was finalized. As in most such proceedings, she won—and she lost. Brenda got primary custody, and on the weekends the children stayed with Chuck and his live-in girlfriend, an arrangement Brenda hated with all her heart.

As for the kids, Jason and Mindy were caught in the middle, where they did indeed suffer—in the short term certainly, and in the long term as well. Both disapproved of what their dad was doing, equal in their distaste for Dinah, but both also were troubled by their mother's bitterness.

Jason, 12 at the time, deeply resented his father's actions, and his relationship with his dad deteriorated as each visitation weekend progressed, almost always culminating in a shouting match between the two by Sunday night.

Mindy, seven, showed her hurt in a different way. She, like many young victims of divorce, believed her parents' breakup was somehow her fault, no matter how much her parents sought to convince her otherwise. If only she would have been a "better little girl," she believed, "Daddy wouldn't have left." And if she tried with all her might to be that better little girl—dressing up in her best clothes for visits to Daddy, being always as pleasant and as positive as she can around him—maybe Daddy would come back home again.

Insecurities and anger at home inevitably flowed over to school. Once the initial flush of anger wore off, Jason developed a premature emotional autonomy to numb his pain, which displayed itself in anti-social and aggressive behavior at school. Mindy, for her part, let the unnatural emotional stress she was under play itself out in depression and then subsequent lashings out at teachers and classmates.

Brenda had to go back to work—for the first time in 12 years. She had no marketable skills and was relegated to answering phones at a department store. The family income that first year was cut by 35 percent. The pressure of supporting herself and her two troubled kids seemed enormous, and she frequently wondered if there wasn't something more she could have done to prevent her marriage from falling apart. There was—but now it was too late.

THE PRUDENT SEE DANGER AND TAKE REFUGE

Proverbs 27:12 is particularly appropriate for marriage. In that passage the wisest of the wise counsels: "The prudent see danger and take refuge, but the simple keep going and suffer for it."

As we have emphasized repeatedly in this book, conflict between persons, even those close to each other, is inevitable. And taking vows to "have and to hold ... for better and for worse ... in sickness and in health ... till death do us part" does not negate the fact that these two people are sinners and will naturally experience conflict, which has the potential to destroy their marriage.

The fact that you are a Christian does not insulate you from these challenges. As hard as it may be to believe, professing Christians have virtually the same divorce rate as those outside the church.[1] Therefore, to think your marriage is somehow immune to divorce because you are a Christian couple is naive.

If spouses are wise, they will heed King Solomon's advice. They will "see danger and take refuge." In other words, they will take deliberate steps to prevent problems and to build into their marriage "insurance policies" that will help them get through troubled times and stay together.

But they will do it *before* the problems arise, when both partners are still committed to making sure their marriage thrives. Brenda in our opening illustration saw the light, all right—but it was too late. Had she and Chuck built insurance into their marriage during their halcyon years together before the kids came along, they would have had a much better chance of making it through the tough times. For once trouble arises, one or both spouses may have second thoughts about the marriage and refuse to make the commitment and do the hard work it takes to preserve their relationship.

Thus it is our goal in this chapter to lay out proactive steps a couple can take to set the stage for dealing with conflict *before* the trouble arises. We will look at seven steps:

- Nurture the marital relationship
- Learn to be peacemakers
- Join a peacemaking church
- Join a couples small group
- Agree to seek help when needed
- Sign a marriage covenant
- Be available to help other couples

Nurture the Marital Relationship

If a marriage is not deliberately nurtured, it will seldom grow and will often deteriorate. As the saying goes, "If you're coasting, you must be going downhill." The attractions, pressures, and temptations of the world can easily pull couples apart. Therefore it is essential that a couple deliberately cultivate the four key dimensions of their marital relationship: spiritual, intellectual/recreational, emotional, and physical.

This book is not about marriage-building per se, but the concept of deliberately nurturing a marriage is so important to preventing marital problems that we must take up this issue briefly.

- *Spiritual.* Two people who draw closer to God will inevitably grow closer to each other. Commit to grow in faith through joint prayer, study of God's Word, corporate worship, and fellowship.

- *Intellectual/recreational.* Commit to mutually enjoying as many relationship-building activities as possible: reading, continuing education, hobbies, entertainment, recreation, sports, travel, hobbies, etc. Doing such activities together enables you to engage each other, share questions and insights, and grow in the same direction.

- *Emotional.* Showing signs of affection, concern, and devotion through words and actions; communicating openly, gently, honestly, and in a way that is sensitive to your spouse's communication style—these are only some of the ways a husband and wife can nurture the emotional bond between them. Especially important in avoiding estrangement and maintaining emotional intimacy are confession and forgiveness—both emotional experiences.

- *Physical.* The sexual relationship extends beyond the bedroom and can be sustained by other displays of affection such as tender touches, hugs, and hand-holding. Physical ardor unites a couple, and need not wane over time; in fact, it can grow steadily if they are willing to keep growing together.

As we mentioned above, this is only the briefest of overviews and is not meant as an exhaustive list of nurturing activities. Many excellent books and seminars are available to help you develop a plan that suits you (see the Digging Deeper section at the end of this chapter).

Learn to Be Peacemakers

As we have seen throughout this book, our sinful natures guarantee conflict within a marriage, no matter how much the individual spouses are committed to each other. It's how spouses *handle* these conflicts that is crucial. If we do not learn how to resolve our differences constructively, the repeated offenses of daily life will accumulate to critical mass and will create a wall that divides or permanently separates us from our spouse.

Reading this book is a great first step in resolving these differences. But you must also commit to practicing what you've learned. As Paul promises in Philippians 4:9, "Whatever you have learned or received or heard from me, or seen in me—put it into practice. And the God of peace will be with you." Conflicts are, in a sense, *opportunities*—chances to practice the biblical principles you've learned in this book.

One great way to practice these principles is to share them with others. Paul says as much in his letter to Philemon: "I pray that you may be active in sharing your faith, so that you will have a full understanding of every good thing we have in Christ" (v. 6). As the verse implies, the more we share what God is teaching us about peacemaking, the more fully we will understand the peacemaking principles.

And one of the best ways to do this is teaching peacemaking skills to others. Anyone who has ever taught a class of any sort—be it from the Bible or in another subject—invariably grows in knowledge of the subject he or she is teaching. The same is true of peacemaking. A good place to start would be by teaching *The Young Peacemaker* to your own children or to the children in your church. You could also volunteer to teach a Sunday school class or small-group Bible study using materials developed by Peacemaker Ministries.[2]

Join a Peacemaking Church

In a survey of two thousand pastors, when asked what was most lacking in their seminary or Bible college training, the top answer was "conflict management."[3] Since many pastors have never learned a practical biblical system for resolving conflicts, it is not surprising that many churches are clumsy and inexperienced when it comes to helping their people resolve conflict.

If things are going well in your marriage, you might never notice this deficiency. But if you encounter severe conflict in your marriage, your church's weakness in this area can make the difference between restoration and divorce.

Therefore one of the best ways to guard your marriage against future catastrophe is to join a church that has deliberately developed its ability to equip and assist its people to respond to conflict in a biblical manner. If you are in a church that does not have this ability, then you should do all you can to encourage the leadership to help the church grow in this area.[4]

Being part of a peacemaking church can help to inspire and encourage you and your spouse to resolve your conflicts biblically. As you see others practicing these principles, you will be encouraged to do the same. For example, if a man in the church gives a testimony about God helping him confess sin to his wife, other husbands may see a similar need in their lives.

When you and your spouse encounter a conflict you cannot resolve on your own, you can turn to other people in the church or church leaders for encouragement, counsel, and accountability to follow through on needed action. And if you or your spouse falls into temptation and will not repent, a church that is committed to peacemaking will follow the process Jesus sets forth in Matthew 18:15-17, through which God often works to restore marriages that seem hopelessly broken (see the story at the end of chapter 11).

Join a Couples Small Group

Early in my marriage, I enjoyed telling others a humorous story about Corlette. She always laughed when I told it, so I thought she enjoyed it as much as I did.

But after hearing me tell the story in a small-group gathering, a friend named Greg asked me out to lunch the next day. He gently confronted me about the story, saying he was concerned that I had hurt Corlette's feelings.

I tried to brush him aside by saying Corlette had always laughed at the story. He countered by saying he was watching her eyes as I told it, and he had seen embarrassment, not laughter. He challenged me to ask her how she really felt about the story.

When I got home, I related my conversation with Greg to her, and ended by saying, "Isn't that silly? He actually thought the story embarrasses you." (That's what we attorneys call a leading question!) Corlette looked at me for a moment and then burst into tears.

"You mean it does embarrass you?" I asked.

"Yes," she replied. "Every time you tell it, I feel like a fool."

I was stunned. "Then why do you always laugh?" I asked.

"Because I don't want to seem overly sensitive," she replied.

I pulled Corlette into my arms and told her how sorry and ashamed I was for being so insensitive toward her. And I promised to ask God to help me be far more careful in the future to watch my words and protect her from embarrassment. I also called Greg to tell him he was right, and to thank him for loving Corlette and me enough to confront me on my sinful behavior.

This story illustrates the wisdom and benefit of deliberately seeking regular close fellowship with other Christian couples who can observe how you interact with your spouse in casual settings and lovingly confront you when they see you doing something that might undermine your marriage.

One of the best ways to find such fellowship is to join a small group where couples study the Bible together and seek to hold one another accountable in their walks with the Lord, especially within their marriages. Such accountability does not happen automatically. Most people are hesitant to confront others, so it is important that the people in your group make an explicit commitment to show their love for one another by living out the accountability principles taught by in Galatians 6:1: "Brothers, if someone is caught in a sin, you who are spiritual should restore him gently" (see also Matthew 18:15-17).[5]

As Christian couples join with one another in small groups to live out God's design for mutual accountability, they can help one another recognize marital problems early on and provide a powerful line of defense against the creeping sin that can destroy our marriages.

Agree to Seek Help When Needed

Another step you can take to protect your marriage is to agree that you will seek outside counsel if you experience marital problems that you cannot resolve on your own. It is important to make this agreement as early as possible, when both of you are committed to your marriage and understand the wisdom and necessity of seeking outside counsel when you cannot resolve differences privately (see Matthew 18:15-16). If you wait until troubles arise to discuss counseling, your spouse may refuse to go to counseling, either because he (or she) is reluctant to admit that he cannot solve his own problems or because he is no longer committed to making the marriage succeed.

When you make this agreement, you should agree on what circumstances will trigger seeking counsel, and who you will go to for help. Here is a model for this type of agreement:

> As Jesus teaches in Matthew 18:15-20, even sincere Christians may not always be able to resolve their differences in private. At times we may need the insight, encouragement, and counsel of other Christians to help us deal with sin and resolve conflict. We recognize that this teaching applies to married couples, and we acknowledge that there may come a time when we need outside assistance in resolving problems that may arise in our marriage or family.
>
> Therefore we commit ourselves before God to jointly seek outside counsel when a conflict between us has gone on for more than 48 hours and either of us does not believe it has been properly resolved. (If either of us acts in a way that might result in physical harm to the other or to anyone else, we agree to seek counsel immediately.)
>
> If we both agree that it is appropriate, we will first seek informal counsel from an individual or couple whom we both recognize as being spiritually mature and able to provide biblically sound advice, such as a personal friend, small-group leader, Sunday school teacher, or church deacon or elder. (If you wish, you may name this person or couple at this time:_____.)
>
> If that person or couple is unavailable or unable to help, we will seek advice from our pastor or from someone he recommends to us. If such counsel does not result in a resolution of our differences, we will seek advice from a Christian counselor, preferably one recommended by our church.
>
> When seeking outside counsel, we recognize that serious problems are seldom resolved in one discussion. Therefore we commit ourselves to continue in counseling as long as it takes to resolve our differences and to be fully reconciled with each other.

Sign a Marriage Covenant

To add further weight to your commitment to guard your marriage and to resolve conflicts in a biblically faithful manner, you may sign a "Christian

Marriage and Peacemaking Covenant" that commits you to turning to the church instead of civil courts to resolve problems that might conceivably give rise to legal issues. This agreement goes as follows:

> Believing that God, in His wisdom and providence, has ordained and established human marriage as a covenant relationship intended to reflect the eternal marriage covenant established through the death, burial and resurrection of His Son with His Church, and therefore human marriage is a sacred and lifelong promise, reflecting our unconditional love for one another, and believing that God intends for the human marriage covenant to reflect His promise never to leave us or forsake us because of what He has done for us through His Son, Jesus Christ, we, the undersigned husband and wife, male and female, made in the image of God, do hereby affirm and reaffirm our solemn pledge to fulfill our marriage vows, so help us God; we furthermore pledge to exalt the sacred nature, glory, and permanence of God's eternal marriage covenant in His Son with the Church through our marriage, by calling others to honor and fulfill their marriage vows; and we, upon full and informed consent and with full knowledge and understanding of this covenant to arbitrate, hereby irrevocably covenant and consent to submit any question concerning whether our marriage should be dissolved to binding arbitration in accordance with the Rules of Procedure of the Institute for Christian Conciliation, a division of Peacemaker Ministries, under the jurisdiction of _____ (name of local church) or any church which we or either one of us might join hereafter, believing that any such issue is strictly a religious question to be resolved solely according to the standards set forth in the Holy Bible, and we do both hereby agree to submit to any arbitration decision made in accordance with the Rules of Procedure of the Institute for Christian Conciliation, a division of Peacemaker Ministries, as final and binding on the question of whether our marriage should be dissolved.[6]

Be Available to Help Other Couples

As God enables you to overcome your own marital challenges and experience a closer and stronger relationship with your spouse, I urge you to make yourself available to help other couples who would benefit from your experience and wisdom.

In many cases, simply being available to have a cup of coffee with someone will open the door for you to give encouragement and guidance that can help a friend resolve basic marital questions before serious problems arise.

If you want to learn more about how to help others deal with marital conflict, I encourage you to enroll in Peacemaker Ministries' Reconciler Training Program (see Appendix E). This training is designed to equip gifted people within the local church with foundational conflict coaching and mediation skills that are directly applicable to marital conflict as well as to other conflicts that Christians encounter in day-to-day life. There is also an advanced training track called "Intervening in Troubled Marriages," which provides further guidance and practice on helping people in troubled marriages.

∎ ∎ ∎

Marriage is a wonderful gift from God, through which He enriches our lives, blesses us with children, guards us against temptation, and presents a model to the world of how Jesus Christ loves His church (Ephesians 5:25). Sin, Satan, and the world conspire daily to oppose God and tarnish this model. Therefore, be wise. Recognize both the opportunities and the dangers that lie ahead. Prepare yourself today to respond to the inevitable conflicts in a biblically faithful manner. As you and your spouse learn how to be peacemakers, you will not only strengthen your marriage, but also turn it into a place where God is glorified, others are served, and both of you are steadily being conformed to the image of the great Peacemaker, our Lord Jesus Christ.

AS YOU GROW

In a fallen world, marriages are inevitably exposed to attack. Disappointed expectations, years of criticism, or attractive alternatives can threaten any marriage. To safeguard your marriage, put these insurance policies into effect today.

1. Nurture your marital relationship at all four levels: spiritual, intellectual/recreational, emotional, and physical.

2. Learn to be peacemakers by repeatedly studying and applying the powerful peacemaking principles set forth in Scripture.

3. Join a peacemaking church where biblical conflict resolution and redemptive discipline is taught, encouraged, and modeled.

4. Join a couples small group where you can share your concerns and burdens and get advice and encouragement from people who really know you.

5. Agree to seek help when needed, specifying when you will look for help and who you will turn to.

6. Sign a marriage covenant that commits you to turn to your church instead of civil courts if your problems become severe.

7. Be available to help other couples. By developing reconciler skills and working with other couples, you can help to preserve other marriages and at the same time learn lessons that will strengthen and guard your marriage.

DIGGING DEEPER

For practical guidance on how to nurture you marriage, see:

▌ *Complete Marriage and Family Home Reference Guide,* by Dr. James Dobson

▌ *Starting Your Marriage Right: What You Need to Know in the Early Years to Make It Last a Lifetime,* by Dennis and Barbara Rainey

▌ *Moments Together for Couples,* by Dennis and Barbara Rainey

▌ *Intimate Issues: Conversations Woman to Woman,* by Linda Dillow and Lorraine Pintus

A Peacemaker's Checklist

Glorify God—*How can I please and honor the Lord in this situation?*

With God's help, I will seek to glorify Him by:
- Constantly looking for ways to give testimony to what Christ has done for me.
- Asking, "What will please and honor God in this situation?"
- Striving earnestly, diligently, and continually to live at peace with my family.
- Remembering that Jesus' reputation is affected by the way I get along with others.
- Trusting that God is always in control and working for my good, even in the midst of conflict.
- Using conflict as an opportunity to serve others.
- Cooperating with God as He prunes me of sinful attitudes, idols, and habits and helps me to grow to be more like Christ.

Get the Log Out of Your Own Eye— *How have I contributed to this conflict, and what do I need to do about it?*

To identify idols that may be ruling my heart, with God's help I will:
- Prayerfully ask myself "X-ray questions" (see page 19) to expose the desires of my heart.
- Keep track of my discoveries in a journal so that I can identify patterns and steadily go after specific idols.
- Pray daily that God would rob my idols of their influence in my life by making me miserable whenever I give in to them.
- Describe my idols to my spouse and an accountability partner, and ask them to pray for me and lovingly confront me when they see signs that the idol is still controlling me.
- Realize that idols are masters of change and disguise. As soon as I gain a victory over a particular demand or form of punishment, my idol is likely to reappear in a related form, with a new justification and more subtle means of judging and punishment.

■ If I am dealing with an idol that is difficult to identify or conquer, I will go to my pastor or some other spiritually mature advisor and seek his or her counsel and support.

■ Most of all, I will ask God to replace my idols with a growing love for Him, and a consuming desire to worship Him and Him alone.

Before talking to others about their wrongs, with God's help I will ask myself:

■ What are the real issues here?

■ Is this something I should simply overlook?

■ Am I guilty of reckless words, falsehood, gossip, or any other worthless talk?

■ Have I kept my word and fulfilled all of my responsibilities?

■ Have I abused my authority?

■ Have I respected those in authority over me?

■ Have I treated others as I would want to be treated?

■ Am I being motivated by desires that I have elevated to demands (idols), and am I judging and punishing others because they are not doing what I want?

When I see that I have sinned, with God's help I will:

■ Repent—that is, change the way I have been thinking so that I turn away from my sin and turn toward God.

■ Confess my sins by using the Seven A's of Confession, namely: addressing everyone I have affected; avoiding *if*, *but*, and *maybe*; admitting specifically what I did wrong; apologizing for hurting others; accepting the consequences of my actions; explaining how I will alter my attitudes and behavior in the future; and asking for forgiveness.

■ Change my attitudes and behavior by: praying for God's help; focusing on the Lord so that I can overcome my personal idols; studying the Bible; and practicing godly character qualities.

Go and Show Your Brother His Fault—*How can I help others to understand how they have contributed to this conflict?*

When I learn that someone has something against me, I will go to that person to talk about it, even if I don't believe I have done anything wrong.

A sin is too serious to overlook if it:

- Is dishonoring God.
- Has damaged our relationship.
- Is hurting or might hurt other people.
- Is hurting the offender and diminishing that person's usefulness to God.

When I need to confront others, with God's help I will:

- Listen responsibly by waiting patiently while others speak, concentrating on what they say, clarifying their comments through appropriate questions, reflecting their feelings and concerns with paraphrased responses, and agreeing with them whenever possible.
- Give hope and encouragement by ministering the gospel (reminding people that Jesus wants to deliver all of us from our sins).
- Choose a time and place that will be conducive to a productive conversation.
- Believe the best about others until I have facts to prove otherwise.
- Talk in person whenever possible.
- Plan my words in advance and try to anticipate how others will respond to me.
- Use "I" statements when appropriate.
- State objective facts rather than personal opinions.
- Use the Bible carefully and tactfully.
- Ask for feedback.
- Offer solutions and preferences.
- Recognize my limits and stop talking once I have said what is reasonable and appropriate.

If I cannot resolve a dispute with someone in private, and if the matter is too serious to overlook, with God's help I will:

- Seek advice on how I can be a more effective peacemaker.
- Suggest to the other person that we seek help from a godly counselor.
- If necessary, arrange on my own for one or two others to talk with us.
- If necessary, seek help from our church and submit to its discipline.

Go and Be Reconciled—*How can I demonstrate forgiveness and encourage a reasonable solution to this conflict?*

When I forgive someone, with God's help I will make these promises:

- I will no longer dwell on this incident.
- I will not bring up this incident again and use it against you.
- I will not talk to others about this incident.
- I will not allow this incident to stand between us or to hinder our personal relationship.

When I am having a difficult time forgiving someone, with God's help I will:

- If necessary, talk with that person to address any unresolved issues and to confirm repentance.
- Renounce the desire to punish the other person, to make that person earn my forgiveness, or to demand guarantees that I will never be wronged again.
- Assess my contributions to the problem.
- Recognize the ways that God is using the situation for good.
- Remember how much God has forgiven me, not only in this situation but also in the past.
- Draw on God's strength through prayer, Bible study, and, if necessary, Christian counseling.

With God's help I will demonstrate forgiveness and practice the replacement principle by:

- Replacing painful thoughts and memories with positive thoughts and memories.
- Saying positive things to and about the person whom I have forgiven.
- Doing loving and constructive things to and for the person whom I have forgiven.

When I need to negotiate an agreement on material issues, with God's help I will PAUSE:

- Prepare thoroughly for our discussions.
- Affirm my respect and concern for the other person.
- Understand the other's interests as well as my own.
- Search for creative solutions that will satisfy as many of our interests as possible.
- Evaluate various options objectively and reasonably.

APPENDIX B

The Young Peacemaker

The curriculum *The Young Peacemaker* presents a powerful system that parents and teachers can use to teach children how to prevent and resolve conflict in a constructive and biblically faithful manner.

The system emphasizes principles of confession, forgiveness, communication, and character development, and uses realistic stories, practical applications, role plays, and stimulating activities. Although the material is designed for 3rd through 7th graders, it has been successfully used with preschool and high school students.

The lessons in *The Young Peacemaker* may be summarized in Twelve Key Principles for Young Peacemakers:

1. Conflict is a slippery slope.
2. Conflict starts in the heart.
3. Choices have consequences.
4. Wise-way choices are better than my-way choices.
5. The blame game makes conflict worse.
6. Conflict is an opportunity.
7. The five A's can resolve conflict.
8. Forgiveness is a choice.
9. It's never too late to start doing what's right.
10. Think before you speak.
11. Respectful communication is more likely to be heard.
12. A respectful appeal can prevent conflict.

This curriculum is designed for use in family devotions, as well as in Sunday school, home school, and Christian school settings. It is also available in a format that is suitable for use in public schools. To order this material, you may visit the Peacemaker Ministries Bookstore on our web site at www.HisPeace.org, or write us at 1537 Avenue D, Suite 352, Billings, MT 59102, or call (406) 256-1583.

Peacemaker Ministries: History and Purpose

The mission of Peacemaker® Ministries is *to equip and assist Christians and their churches to respond to conflict biblically.*

The ministry was founded in 1982 by a group of pastors, lawyers, and business people who wanted to encourage and assist Christians to respond to conflict biblically. Since then we have developed educational resources, seminars, and conciliation training to help Christians learn how to serve God as peacemakers in the conflicts they encounter in everyday life.

Through our international network of conciliators, we also provide conflict counseling, mediation, and arbitration services to help resolve personal conflicts, business disputes, church and ministry divisions, and even complicated lawsuits.

REFERRALS TO LOCAL CONCILIATORS

If you encounter a conflict in your family that you are unable to resolve personally, follow Jesus' teaching in Matthew 18:16 by seeking aid from someone in your community. You should start by asking whether there is someone in your church or a neighboring church who has demonstrated a particular gift for peacemaking. Many churches are training such people through our Reconciler Training Program. If you are unable to locate a qualified reconciler in a local church, you may contact Peacemaker Ministries and ask for the names of any Certified Christian Conciliators™ in your area.

EQUIPPING YOUR CHURCH FOR PEACEMAKING

One of our primary goals is to assist churches in developing a "culture of peace" where people can experience peace and find practical guidance on resolving conflict. There are several steps that a church can take to create an environment where members are consistently encouraged and assisted to respond to conflict biblically. These steps include:

- Educating adults on peacemaking through Sunday school classes and small group Bible studies (see Appendix D for useful resources).
- Educating children through family devotions and Sunday school classes using *The Young Peacemaker* (see Appendix B).
- Amending church bylaws to specifically incorporate peacemaking principles, including the use of redemptive church discipline (see *Managing Conflict in Your Church* materials in Appendix D).
- Training gifted members to serve the congregation as reconcilers (see Appendix E).

For more specific guidance on how to develop a culture of peace in your church, visit our Web site at HisPeace.org, and click on "Equip the Church." Additional resources and information about Peacemaker Ministries are available on our Web site, or you may write us at 1537 Avenue D, Suite 352, Billings, MT 59102, or call (406) 256-1583.

Peacemaking Resources

Peacemaker Ministries has developed an array of resources that you can use to teach and practice biblical peacemaking. Our most popular resources include:

- ▌ *The Peacemaker: A Biblical Guide to Resolving Personal Conflict* (Baker Books, 2nd ed. 1997) provides a comprehensive discussion of the biblical principles you can use to resolve everything from simple personal offenses to family and marital conflicts, church divisions, and business and legal disputes.
- ▌ The Leader's Guide for *Responding to Conflict Biblically* provides detailed guidance on how to teach biblical peacemaking in a Sunday school setting.
- ▌ *Peacemaking* Small Group Member's Guide is geared toward the intimacy and accountability associated with small groups. This 13-part curriculum is ideal for interactive and discussion-oriented groups of 12 or less.
- ▌ PeaceSowers™ Discipleship Course Instructor's Manual: This 12-week course is an alternative to our Sunday school material and is designed for groups who want to study peacemaking in greater depth. Modeled after Dr. James Kennedy's Evangelism Explosion™, it requires outside reading, memory work, and practical application of peacemaking principles in actual conflicts.
- ▌ *The Young Peacemaker* is designed for parents and teachers who want to teach peacemaking to children. The set includes a Parent/Teacher Manual, Student Activity Booklets, and a license to reproduce the stories and activity sheets from the Student Activity Booklets.
- ▌ *Managing Conflict in Your Church* provides special training for church leaders on how to counsel members in conflict, mediate disputes, practice redemptive church discipline, and reduce exposure to legal liability through improved bylaws, membership policies, and youth worker screening. The set includes six

hours of audiotapes and a 220-page study manual. Eighty pages of the manual are model letters, forms, and policies that are also on an enclosed floppy diskette.

▮ **Guiding People through Conflict** is a quick-to-read 48-page booklet that demonstrates how you can help other people resolve conflict through Christian reconciliation. Six short stories from actual cases illustrate how mature Christians guided others through disputes using conflict counseling, mediation, and arbitration. The Mediator's Checklist guides you through opening statements, storytelling, problem-solving, and leading others to agreement.

For information on additional educational resources, please visit the Bookstore on our Web site at www.HisPeace.org, write us at 1537 Avenue D, Suite 352, Billings, MT 59102, or call (406) 256-1583.

APPENDIX E

Peacemaker Ministries' Reconciler Training Program

The Reconciler Training Program is designed to equip you to minister the Lord's peace in a wide array of conflict situations. It prepares you to resolve not only significant material issues but also the complex personal issues that fuel human conflict. Through this training, you can learn biblical principles and skills essential for biblical conflict coaching and mediation. The first part of the program, the Reconciler Course, is useful to church and ministry leaders, business managers, administrators, attorneys, teachers, counselors, and anyone else who wants to give sound biblical advice to others in conflict.

The Reconciler Course includes the following materials:

> *The Peacemaker* (book)
> Peacemaker Seminar (tapes and manual)
> Christian Conciliation Procedures Course (tapes and manual)
> Changing Hearts, Changing Lives Course (tapes and manual)
> Guidelines for Christian Conciliation

The second part of the Reconciler Training Program is the Reconciler Practicum, a two-day event that lets you put peacemaking theory into practice. As you work through a mediation step-by-step and gain experience by participating in mediations based on actual cases, you'll build confidence in what God can do through you to help people in conflict. You'll be able to offer help and hope to people in conflict.

Individuals who complete both the Reconciler Course and the Reconciler Practicum are eligible to attend advanced training events, such as Intervening in Marriage Conflict and Intervening in Church Conflict.

The Cross and Criticism

This article originally appeared in the Spring 1999 issue of *The Journal of Biblical Counseling*, (Vol. 17, No. 3) and is reprinted by permission.

On January 28, 1986, the space shuttle *Challenger* and its crew embarked on a mission to broaden educational horizons and promote the advancement of scientific knowledge. The most outstanding objective of the *Challenger* 51-L mission was the delivery of educational lessons from space by teacher Christa McAuliffe. A lesson was, indeed, delivered, but not one which anyone expected.

Just 75 seconds after liftoff, tragedy struck. Before a watching world the shuttle suddenly erupted overhead, disintegrating the cabin along with its crew. The debris of metal, blood and bones plummeted to earth, along with our nation's glory.

What had gone wrong? That was the pressing question everyone asked. As teams of researchers examined the wreckage, the specific cause was soon found. The problem was with the O-rings (circular rubber seals), which had been designed to fit snugly into the joints of the booster engine sections. Evidently, the O-rings had become defective under adverse conditions, and the resulting mechanical failure led to the tragedy. Was that the whole story?

The truth eventually got out. The *New York Times* put it frankly: the ultimate cause of the space shuttle disaster was *pride*. A group of top managers failed to listen carefully to the warnings, advice and criticisms given by those down the line who were concerned about the operational reliability of certain parts of the booster engine under conditions of abnormal stress. Just think: *heeding criticism could have saved seven human lives*.

As a pastor, church leader, and lecturer for Peacemaker Ministries, I am blessed with the opportunity to minister to people and congregations in conflict. Among the many things I've come to learn is the dominant role that giving and taking criticism has in exacerbating conflict. Yet, even more, I've learned that the remedy wonderfully provided by God requires us to return to the cross of Christ. For our present purposes, I want us to look at the problem of *taking* criticism.

The Dynamic of Defending Against Criticism

First of all, let me define what I mean by criticism. I'm using criticism in a broad sense as referring to *any judgment made about you by another, which declares that you fall short of a particular standard.* The standard may be God's or man's. The judgment may be true or false. It may be given gently with a view to correction, or harshly and in a condemnatory fashion. It may be given by a friend or by an enemy. But whatever the case, it is a judgment or criticism about you, that you have fallen short of a standard.

However it comes, most of us would agree that criticism is difficult to take. Who of us doesn't know someone with whom we need to be especially careful in our remarks lest they blow up in response to our suggested corrections? Unfortunately, as I travel around the country, the tale is often told that many people would never dare confront or criticize their pastor or leader for fear of retaliation. Many just find another organization to work for or church to attend.

In fact, don't you know of leaders who select those to be nearest to them who are easiest on them? How many times have you been warned to "walk on eggshells" around that person?

As sad a commentary as this is, such people are not much different from me. I, too, do not like criticism. Any criticism is hard for me to take. I'd much rather be commended than corrected, praised than rebuked. I'd much rather judge than be judged! And I do not think that I am alone in this. The more I listen, the more I hear the dynamic of defensiveness against criticism.

In counseling, I see it in the humorous way a couple will be diverted from the issue at hand to debate who said what, when, and where. Or in how people debate back and forth as to whether it was a Tuesday or a Wednesday when they did something.

Why do we expend so much time and energy swatting at these flies with sledgehammers? Why are our hearts and minds so instantly engaged and our emotions surging with great vigor in our defense? The answer is simple. These issues are not minor or insignificant. We defend that which we deem of great value. We think it is our *life* we are saving. We believe something much larger will be lost if we do not use every means to rescue it. *Our name, our reputation, our honor, our glory.*

"If *I* don't point out that *I've* been misunderstood, misquoted, or falsely accused, then others won't know *I'm right*. And if *I* don't point out *my* rightness, nobody will. *I* will be scorned and condemned in the eyes of others."

Do you see the *idol of self* here? The desire for self-justification? But idols have legs. Because of this deep idolatrous desire for self-justification, the tragedy of the Space Shuttle gets played out over and over again in our relationships. It destroys our ability to listen and learn, and it provokes us to quarrel.

Thus, for the sake of our pride and foolishness, we willingly suffer loss of friends, spouse, or loved ones. Some of that destruction comes in the shape of a thin truce. We tolerate a cold war. We make a false peace. We pledge to each other to discuss only those things which have little significance for bettering our souls. We lay out land mines and threaten the other that we will explode in anger if they so much as raise the forbidden subject of my mistake, my error, or my sin.

This is how churches split and factions develop. We surround ourselves with "yes" men—people willing to never challenge, advise, or criticize us. Yet, while we go on defending ourselves against criticism, we find Scripture teaching something different.

Criticism Commended

The ability to hear and heed correction or criticism is commended in Scripture, particularly in Proverbs. Being teachable, able and willing to receive correction, is a mark of the wise. And the wise father or mother will encourage as well as model such an attitude for their daughters and sons.

The way of a fool seems right to him, but a wise man *listens to advice* (Prov. 12:15).

Pride only breeds quarrels, but wisdom is found in those who *take advice* (Prov. 13:10).

A rebuke *impresses* a man of discernment more than a hundred lashes a fool (Prov. 17:10).

The ability to take advice, correction, and rebuke is not only considered a *mark* of the wise, and the inability a *mark* of the fool, but both the wise and the fool *reap* according to their ability to take criticism:

He who scorns instruction *will pay for it*, but he who respects a command is *rewarded* (Prov. 13:13).

Instruct a wise man and he *will be wiser still*; teach a righteous man and he *will add to his learning* (Prov. 9:9).

He who ignores discipline despises himself, but whoever heeds correction *gains understanding* (Prov. 15:32).

There is *gain* in taking criticism. No wonder David exclaims in Psalm 141:5: Let a righteous man strike me—it is a *kindness*; let him rebuke me—it is *oil on my head*. My head *will not refuse it*. David knows the profit of gaining wisdom, knowledge, and understanding. He knows rebukes are a kindness, a blessing, an honor.

Ask yourself: Is that how you look at a rebuke? Is that how you perceive criticism, correction or counsel? Do you want to look at it that way?

How can we move from always being quick to defend ourselves against any and all criticism toward becoming instead like David who saw it as gain? The answer is through understanding, believing, and affirming all that God says about us in the cross of Christ.

Paul summed it up when he said, "I have been crucified with Christ." A believer is one who identifies with all that God affirms and condemns in Christ's crucifixion. God affirms in Christ's crucifixion the whole truth about Himself: His holiness, goodness, justice, mercy, and truth as revealed and demonstrated in His Son, Jesus. Equally, in the cross God condemns the lie: sin, deceit, and the idolatrous heart. He condemns my sinfulness as well as my specific sins. Let's see how this applies to giving and taking criticism.

First, in Christ's Cross I Agree With God's *Judgment* of Me

I see myself as God sees me—a sinner. There is no escaping the truth: "No one is righteous, not even one" (Rom. 3:9-18). In response to my sin, the cross has criticized and judged me more intensely, deeply, pervasively, and truly than anyone else ever could. This knowledge permits us to say to all other criticism of us: "This is just a fraction of it."

Cursed is everyone who does not continue to do everything written in the Book of the Law (Gal. 3:10).

For whoever keeps the whole law and yet stumbles at just one point is guilty of breaking all of it (James 2:10).

By faith, I affirm God's judgment of myself, that I am a sinner. I also believe that the answer to my sin lies in the cross.

I have been crucified with Christ and I no longer live (Gal. 2:20).

For we know that our old self was crucified with him [Jesus] so that the body of sin might be done away with, that we should no longer be slaves to sin (Rom. 6:6).

If the cross says anything, it speaks about my sin. The person who says "I have been crucified with Christ" is a person well aware of his sinfulness. You'll never get life right by your own unaided efforts because all who rely on observing the law are under a curse. "Cursed is *everyone* who does not continue to do *everything* written in the Book of the Law" (Gal. 3:10). Thus the cross doesn't merely criticize or judge us; it condemns us for not doing *everything* written in God's law. Do you believe that? Do you feel the force of that criticism? Do you appreciate the thoroughness of God's judgment?

The crucified person also knows that he cannot defend himself against God's judgment by trying to offset his sin by his good works. Think about this fact: whoever keeps the whole law and yet stumbles at just one point is guilty of breaking all of it (James 2:10).

To claim to be a Christian is to agree with all God says about our sin. As a person "crucified with Christ," we admit, agree, and approve of God's judgment against us: There is no one righteous, not even one (Rom. 3:10).

Second, In Christ's Cross I Agree With God's *Justification* of Me

I must not only agree with God's judgment of me as sinner in the cross of Christ, but I must also agree with God's justification of me as sinner. Through the sacrificial love of Jesus, God justifies ungodly people (Rom. 3:21-26).

But the life I now live, I live by faith in the Son of God who loved me and gave himself for me (Gal. 2:20).

My goal is to boast in Christ's righteousness, not my own.

No one will be declared righteous in his [God's] sight by observing the law (Rom. 3:20).

This righteousness from God comes through faith in Jesus Christ to all who believe (Rom. 3:22).

Pride breeds quarrels, says Solomon. Quarrels are often over who is right. Quarrels erupt in our idolatrous demand for self-justification. But not if I am applying the cross. For the cross not only declares God's just verdict against me as a sinner, but His declaration of righteousness by grace through faith in Christ.

The cross of Christ reminds me that the Son of God loved me and gave Himself for me. And because of this, God has thoroughly and forever accepted me in Christ. Here is how grace works: Christ redeemed us from the curse of the law by becoming a curse for us, for it is written: "Cursed is everyone who is hung on a tree." He redeemed us in order that the blessing given to Abraham might come to the Gentiles through Christ Jesus, so that by faith we might receive the promise of the Spirit (Gal. 3:13f).

What a sure foundation for the soul! Now, I don't practice self-justification, but boasting—boasting about Christ's righteousness for me.

If you truly take this to heart, the whole world can stand against you, denounce you, or criticize you, and you will be able to reply, "If God has justified me, who can condemn me?" "If God justifies me, accepts me, and will never forsake me, then why should I feel insecure and fear criticism?" "Christ took my sins, and I receive His Spirit. Christ takes my condemnation, and I receive His righteousness."

Implications for Dealing with Criticism

In light of God's judgment and justification of the sinner in the cross of Christ, we can begin to discover how to deal with any and all criticism. By agreeing with God's criticism of me in Christ's cross, I can face any criticism man may lay against me. In other words, no one can criticize me more than the cross has. And the most devastating criticism turns out to be the finest mercy. If you thus know yourself as having been crucified with Christ, then you can respond to any criticism, even mistaken or hostile criticism, without bitterness, defensiveness, or blameshifting. Such responses typically exacerbate and intensify conflict, and lead to the rupture of relationships. You can learn to hear criticism as constructive and not condemnatory because God has justified you.

Who will bring any charge against those whom God has chosen? It is God who justifies. Who is he that condemns? (Rom. 8:33-34a).

Let a righteous man strike me—it is a kindness; let him rebuke me—it is oil on my head. My head will not refuse it (Ps. 141:5).

If I know myself as crucified with Christ, I can now receive another's criticism with this attitude: "You have not discovered a fraction of my guilt. Christ has said more about my sin, my failings, my rebellion and my foolishness than any man can lay against me. I thank you for your corrections. They are a blessing and a kindness to me. For even when they are wrong or misplaced, they remind me of my true faults and sins for which my Lord and Savior paid dearly when He went to the cross for me. I want to hear where your criticisms are valid."

The correction and advice that we hear are sent by our heavenly Father. They are His corrections, rebukes, warnings, and scoldings. His reminders are meant to humble me, to weed out the root of pride and replace it with a heart and lifestyle of growing wisdom, understanding, goodness, and truth. For example, if you can take criticism—however just or unjust—you'll learn to give it with gracious intent and constructive results. See section below, "*Giving Criticism God's Way.*"

I do not fear man's criticism for I have already agreed with God's criticism. And I do not look ultimately for man's approval for I have gained by grace God's approval. In fact, His love for me helps me to hear correction and criticism as a kindness, oil on my head, from my Father who loves me and says, "My son, do not make light of the Lord's discipline, and do not lose heart when He rebukes you, because the Lord disciplines those he loves, and he punishes everyone He accepts as a son" (Heb. 12:5-6).

Applying What We've Learned

1. *Critique yourself.* How do I typically react to correction? Do I pout when criticized or corrected? What is my first response when someone says I'm wrong? Do I tend to attack the person? To reject the content of criticism? To react to the manner? How well do I take advice? How well do I seek it? Are people able to approach me to correct me? Am I teachable?

Do I harbor anger against the person who criticizes me? Do I immediately seek to defend myself, hauling out my righteous acts and personal opinions in order to defend myself and display my rightness? Can my spouse, parents, children, brothers, sisters, or friends correct me?

2. *Ask the Lord to give you a desire to be wise instead of a fool.* Use Proverbs to commend to yourself the goodness of being willing and able to receive criticism, advice, rebuke, counsel, or correction. Meditate upon the passages given above: Proverbs 9:9; 12:15; 13:10,13; 15:32; 17:10; Psalm 141:5.

3. *Focus on your crucifixion with Christ.* While I can say I have faith in Christ, and even say with Paul, "I have been crucified with Christ,"

yet I still find myself not living in light of the cross. So I challenge myself with two questions. First, if I continually squirm under the criticism of others, how can I say I know and agree with the criticism of the cross? Second, if I typically justify myself, how can I say I know, love, and cling to God's justification of me through Christ's cross? This drives me back to contemplating God's judgment and justification of the sinner in Christ on the cross. As I meditate on what God has done in Christ for me, I find a resolve to agree with and affirm all that God says about me in Christ, with whom I've been crucified.

4. *Learn to speak nourishing words to others.* I want to receive criticism as a sinner living within Jesus' mercy, so how can I *give* criticism in a way that communicates mercy to another? Accurate, balanced criticism, given mercifully, is the easiest to hear—and even against that my pride rebels. Unfair criticism or harsh criticism (whether fair or unfair) is needlessly hard to hear. How can I best give accurate, fair criticism, well tempered with mercy and affirmation?

My prayer is that in your struggle against the sin of self-justification you will deepen your love for the glory of God as revealed in the gospel of His Son, and that you will grow wise by faith.

Giving Criticism God's Way

I see my brother/sister as one for whom Christ died (1 Cor. 8:11).
Keep on loving each other as brothers (Heb. 13:1).

I come as an equal, who also is a sinner.
Are we any better than they? Not at all. For there is no one righteous...for all have sinned and fall short of the glory of God (Rom. 3:9,23).

I prepare my heart lest I speak out of wrong motives.
All a man's ways seem innocent to him, but motives are weighed by the LORD (Prov. 16:2).

The heart of the righteous weighs its answers, but the mouth of the wicked gushes evil (Prov. 15:28).

A wise man's heart guides his mouth, and his lips promote instruction (Prov. 16:23).

I examine my own life and confess my sin first.
Why do you look at the speck of sawdust in your brother's eye and pay no attention to the plank in your own eye? How can you say to your brother, "Let me take the speck out of your eye," when all the

time there is a plank in your own eye? You hypocrite, first take the plank out of your own eye, and then you will see clearly to remove the speck from your brother's eye (Matt. 7:3-5).

I am always patient, in it for the long haul (Eph. 4:2).

Love is patient, love is kind. It does not envy, it does not boast, it is not proud. (1 Cor. 13:4).

My goal is not to condemn by debating points, but to build up through constructive criticism.

Do not let any unwholesome talk come out of your mouths, but only what is helpful for building others up according to their needs, that it may give grace to those who listen (Eph. 4:29).

I correct and rebuke my brother gently, in the hope that God will grant him the grace of repentance even as I myself repent only through His grace.

And the Lord's servant must not quarrel; instead, he must be kind to everyone, able to teach, not resentful. Those who oppose him he must gently instruct, in the hope that God will grant them repentance leading them to a knowledge of the truth... (2 Tim. 2:24-25).

■ ■ ■

Alfred J. Poirier pastors Rocky Mountain Community Church, OPC, as well as serves as adjunct instructor for Peacemaker Ministries on issues involving conflict counseling and mediation. He is a D. Min. candidate in counseling at Westminster Theological Seminary in Glenside, PA.

ENDNOTES

Chapter 1
1. The "Slippery Slope" is adapted from *The Peacemaker: A Biblical Guide to Resolving Personal Conflict*; see p. 17-24.

Chapter 2
1. I owe Paul Tripp, David Powlison, and Ed Welch of the Christian Counseling and Educational Foundation (www.CCEF.org) a great debt for the many insights they have given to me on this topic through their books and seminars.
2. F. Samuel Janzow, *Luther's Large Catechism: A Contemporary Translation with Study Questions* (St. Louis: Concordia Publishing House, 1978), p. 13.
3. *Journal on Biblical Counseling* 16, no. 1, fall 1997.
4. John Piper, *Future Grace* (Sisters, Ore: Multnomah), page 9.

Chapter 6
1. C. S. Lewis, *Mere Christianity* (New York: Macmillan, 1960), p. 116.

Chapter 10
1. For more guidance on how to love people who seem intent on hurting you, see chapter 12 in *The Peacemaker*.

Chapter 11
1. See pages 177-78 in *The Peacemaker* for a true story of how the threat of church discipline motivated a man to give up an affair and return to his wife.

Chapter 12
1. The Barna Research Group, Ltd., August 6, 2001, Survey on Divorce, Marriage, and Remarriage.
2. Peacemaker Ministries has developed educational, Sunday school, and small group study materials for children and adults. See Appendix D or visit our Web site at www.HisPeace.org.
3. "Your Church," March/April, 1995, p. 56.

4. See Appendix C for guidance on how a church can improve its ability to equip and assist its members to respond to conflict biblically.

5. For excellent guidance on how to establish a small group with meaningful accountability commitments, see C. J. Mahaney's book *Why Small Groups?*, published by PDI, 7501 Muncaster Mill Rd., Gaithersburg, MD 20877; ph: (301) 926-2200.

6. The "Christian Marriage and Peacemaking Covenant" was developed by David Sims at FamilyLife in cooperation with Peacemaker Ministries. Legal enforceability of the covenant will vary from state to state, so it should be used only after consulting with a local attorney. Even in states where it is not enforceable, however, it may provide your church with additional incentive to use discipline to discourage an unbiblical divorce. For more information on the covenant and a comprehensive related article, "Reclaiming the Church's Jurisdiction over Marriage," go to www.FamilyLife.com, and click on "The Christian Marriage Covenant."

BIBLIOGRAPHY

Chapman, Gary. *Hope for the Separated*. Chicago: Moody Press, 1982.

Dillow, Linda, and Lorraine Pintus. *Intimate Issues: Conversations Woman to Woman*. Colorado Springs: WaterBrook Press, 1999.

Dobson, Dr. James. *Complete Marriage and Family Home Reference Guide*. Wheaton: Tyndale House, 2000.

Dobson, Dr. James. *Love Must Be Tough*. Dallas: Word Publishing, 1983, 1996.

Dobson, Dr. James. *The New Dare to Discipline*. Wheaton: Tyndale House, 1970, 1992.

Dobson, Dr. James. *Parenting Isn't for Cowards*. Dallas: Word Publishing, 1987.

Fitzpatrick, Elyse. *Idols of the Heart: Learning to Long for God Alone*. Phillipsburg: P&R, 2001.

Piper, John. *Future Grace*. Sisters, Ore: Multnomah, 1995.

Rainey, Dennis and Barbara. *Moments Together for Couples*. Ventura, Calif.: Regal Books, 1995.

Rainey, Dennis and Barbara. *Starting Your Marriage Right: What You Need to Know in the Early Years to Make It Last a Lifetime*. Nashville: Thomas Nelson, 2000.

Sande, Corlette. *The Young Peacemaker: Teaching Students to Respond to Conflict God's Way*. Wapwallopen: Shepherd Press, 1997.

Sande, Ken. *Managing Conflict in Your Church*. Billings: Peacemaker Ministries, 1993, 1999.

Sande, Ken. *The Peacemaker: A Biblical Guide to Resolving Personal Conflict.* Grand Rapids: Baker Books, 2nd Edition, 1997.

Sande, Ken; Lee, Dr. Jimmy Ray, and Brad Rymer. *Peacemaking: Responding to Conflict Biblically, a Small Group Bible Study.* Chattanooga: Turning Point Ministries, 2000.

Tripp, Paul David *Age of Opportunity: A Biblical Guide to Parenting Teens.* Phillipsburg: P&R, 1997.

Tripp, Paul. *War of Words.* Phillipsburg: P&R, 1999.

Tripp, Tedd. *Shepherding a Child's Heart.* Wapwallopen: Shepherd Press, 1995.

Welch, Edward. *Addictions: A Banquet in the Grave.* Phillipsburg: P&R, 2001.

Welch, Edward. *When People Are Big and God Is Small: Overcoming Peer Pressure, Codependency, and the Fear of Man.* Phillipsburg: P&R, 1997.

FOCUS ON THE FAMILY®
Welcome to the *Family!*

Whether you received this book as a gift, borrowed it from a friend, or purchased it yourself, we're glad you read it! It's just one of the many helpful, insightful, and encouraging resources produced by Focus on the Family.

In fact, that's what Focus on the Family is all about—providing inspiration, information, and biblically based advice to people in all stages of life.

It began in 1977 with the vision of one man, Dr. James Dobson, a licensed psychologist and author of 16 best-selling books on marriage, parenting, and family. Alarmed by the societal, political, and economic pressures that were threatening the existence of the American family, Dr. Dobson founded Focus on the Family with one employee—an assistant—and a once-a-week radio broadcast, aired on only 36 stations.

Now an international organization, Focus on the Family is dedicated to preserving Judeo-Christian values and strengthening the family through more than 70 different ministries, including eight separate daily radio broadcasts; television public service announcements; 10 publications; and a steady series of books and award-winning films and videos for people of all ages and interests.

Recognizing the needs of, as well as the sacrifices and important contributions made by, such diverse groups as educators, physicians, attorneys, crisis pregnancy center staff, and single parents, Focus on the Family offers specific outreaches to uphold and minister to these individuals, too. And it's all done for one purpose, and one purpose only: to encourage and strengthen individuals and families through the life-changing message of Jesus Christ.

•   •   •

For more information about the ministry, or if we can be of help to your family, simply write to Focus on the Family, Colorado Springs, CO 80995 or call 1-800-A-FAMILY (1-800-232-6459). Friends in Canada may write Focus on the Family, P.O. Box 9800, Stn. Terminal, Vancouver, B.C. V6B 4G3, or call 1-800-661-9800. Visit our Web site—www.family.org—to learn more about Focus on the Family or to find out if there is an associate office in your country.

We'd love to hear from you!

Lifesavers for Families!
From Focus on the Family®

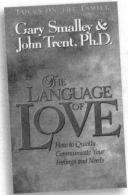

The Language of Love

"Why can't he understand how I feel?" a wife asks herself in desperation after another failed attempt to communicate with her husband. Communication frustrations affect not only our marriages but also our friendships, parent-child and professional relationships. In The Language of Love, Gary Smalley and John Trent explore "emotional word pictures," a time-tested method of bridging communication gaps. The "language of love" can help capture another's attention, make our messages memorable, open the door to greater intimacy, and bring about lasting change!

Guiding Your Family in a Misguided World

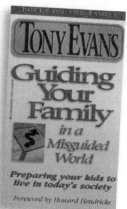

Despite the negative forces in our society, you can claim God's promises for your family and stand strong. Written by Tony Evans, respected pastor, popular Promise Keeper speaker, and father of four, Guiding Your Family in a Misguided World offers practical suggestions for creating a stable, Christ-centered home. Parents will be shown ways to help them and their children develop strong faith and God-honoring lives.

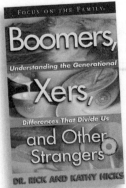

Boomers, Xers, and Other Strangers

Ever wondered why some people seem so different in their lifestyles, values, and opinions? Chances are, it's largely because of what was happening in the world as they grew up. In Boomers, Xers, and Other Strangers, the authors present a fascinating look at what shaped each generation, as well as how we can appreciate each other for the unique wisdom and strengths that define these unique age groups.

• • •

Look for these special books in your local Christian bookstore—
or you may request them from us. Either log on to www.family.org or call
Focus on the Family toll-free at 1-800-A-FAMILY (1-800-232-6459).
Friends in Canada can call 1-800-661-9800.